D1073358

Other books by Dr. Pat Allen:

"Getting to I Do"
"Staying Married and Loving It"
"The Truth About Men Will Set You Free...
but first it'll p*ss you off!"

For more information on Dr. Pat Allen, visit www.drpatallen.com.

To order your copy of "The Answers" DVD, as well as other Dr. Pat Allen books and products, visit Amazon.com, drpatallen.com, or purchase the items at any Dr. Allen event.

Compiled and Edited by Barbara Schroeder

Dedicated to all who endeavor to live and love better.

Introduction

The setting: A balmy evening in northern California.

The crowd of thousands is waiting anxiously, the excitement clearly building. Finally, the moment arrives and Dr. Pat Allen takes center stage. Oblivious to the thunderous applause, she trains a steady gaze upon the audience, commanding their undivided attention.

"Is anyone in pain?" she asks, "Anyone have problems?"

"Yes," murmurs the crowd, eager for a prescription.

"Well" she continues, "I don't care. That's right, I don't care about your feelings of pain."

The shift in mood is palpable; the quizzical look on one man's face speaks volumes. What did she just say? "I said, I don't care about your feelings of pain."

She stands firm in the moment, then at the last minute, delivers the stroke, "What I care about is getting you out of pain. Listen carefully to what I say: Pain is an indicator of change needed or change in progress. Pain is *not* a reason to *not* grow up."

Dr. Allen moves closer to the audience, "Your feelings are authentic, and I appreciate them. But unless they render you absolutely helpless, I want you to walk through them. Don't avoid them, don't get drunk, use drugs or act out. Plow through the feelings. Practice stoicism. He or she who pushes the arrow through gets to move on."

The crowd gets it. This is what they came here for, clear truths, no psychobabble.

"I'm not here to find out why you did or didn't do it, consider what you've done a bad habit. I'm here to help you get out of that habit. But I will not be seduced by your pain to enable you to continue playing your games."

"And remember this," Dr. Allen continues, "I refuse to judge you, or judge what you did that brought you to this point. I'm not a moralist. I'm a therapist. I care about moving you forward. So let's begin the process. Here is your mantra:

The way out of any negative feeling is a positive decision followed by action as soon as possible. That is your mantra, from me to you. When you have any discomfort, any pain, think of that phrase..."

The audience is riveted, ready to experience for themselves why "The Secret" phenomenon's Bob Proctor calls Dr. Allen, "The best expert in personal communications I've ever come across."

Licensed as a marriage and family therapist with a specialty in addictions, Dr. Allen has been assisting people find ways to live and love better for over 30 years.

This collection of questions, answers and personal stories is also featured on the DVD called, "The Answers from Dr. Pat Allen." The contents of both this book and the DVD were assembled from hundreds of Dr. Allen's seminars, private sessions and her signature Monday night improv stage therapy shows in Los Angeles. Her devoted fans have been asking for a written treasure trove of her best advice, and here it is.

If you're new to Dr. Allen's work, welcome! Now it's your turn to experience the wit and wisdom of an iconic therapist who's been called "the dad you never had, and a mother like no other."

Let the questioning begin!

The Answers Book

From Dr. Pat Allen

Compiled and edited by Barbara Schroeder

Table of Contents

CHAPTER 1: WHY DOES MY LIFE SUCK?

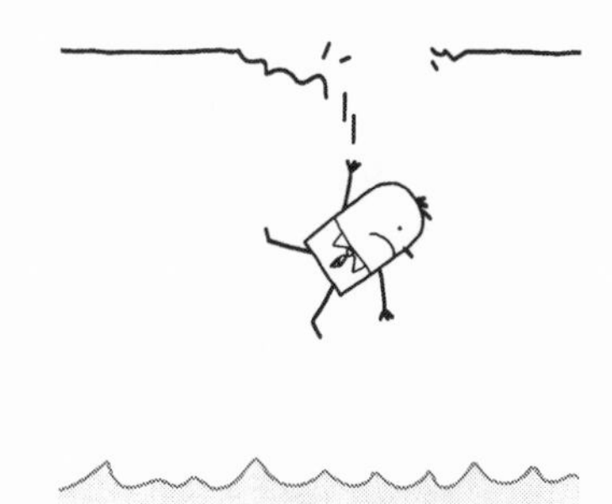

CHAPTER 2: WHY DON'T I HAVE A GREAT RELATIONSHIP?

CHAPTER 3: HOW CAN I TELL IF IT'S REALLY LOVE?

CHAPTER 4: THE 20 FAQs

CHAPTER 5: FAMOUS DR. PAT ALLEN GEMS

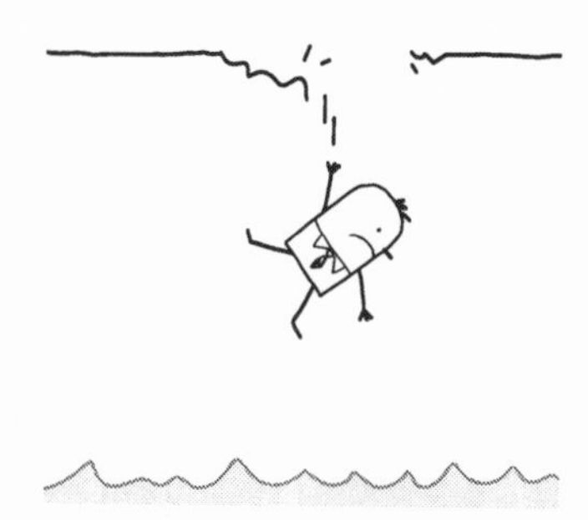

CHAPTER 1: WHY DOES MY LIFE SUCK?

Do you ever react first, and think later? Are you obsessing about a problem or person? Can't find a solution? Don't like the way someone's talking to you but you can't respond effectively? Hurting someone you love?

Most people, instead of communicating in a healthy way, play verbal intimidation games, or verbal seduction games. They react to life based upon what other people have taught them and they criticize themselves and others.

The key to communicating more effectively, as Dr. Allen likes to say, is to "Watch your mouth!"

So maybe your life sucks because...

YOU ARE A COMMUNICATION LOSER

There are 4 ways Dr. Allen says people speak that will reveal if they're a bad communicator. Communication losers are:

1. **Condescending:** This would be someone saying things like "Oh come on, you should know that," or any "I'm ok, you're not ok" kind of comment.

2. **Abrupt:** These are people who say "shut up" or suddenly hang up on you, or maybe just stomp away during a discussion.

3. **Secretive:** An example of this is someone saying, "If you really loved me, you would have known," even though they never told you what you should have known. You're being asked to be a mind reader. This category includes people who really are just keeping secrets from you.

4. **Evasive:** This is someone who's dodging issues and questions, perhaps someone who is hard to pin down, saying things like "I'll marry you. Someday." Or "I'll deal with this later."

YOU REACT INSTEAD OF THINKING FIRST

Dr. Allen says there are only two ways to react to someone or something: emotionally or rationally. She adds that there's a strange phenomenon associated with this theory: that rational people care about feelings and emotional people *don't* care about feelings.

Her explanation: Emotional people (the majority of us) do a feel, react, think routine, where you feel your pain or pleasure, react on that feeling and then think later.

Rational people do the opposite: feel, think, react. You feel your pain or pleasure, figure out what you want and don't want, think about the cost factor, and only then act on it.

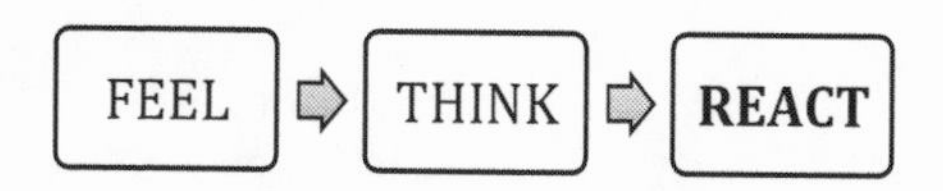

A quote from Dr. Allen, "Now if you really want to make the industry of shrink-dom powerful and rich, here's what you gotta do: feel, think, feel, think, feel, think. What's that called? Rumination! You can stop rumination by going back to your main mantra: The way out of a negative feeling is a positive decision (what do I want or what do I not want) followed by action or inaction as soon as possible."

*Note: Your action may actually be the decision to *not* react (inaction), as in "I'm consciously deciding not to react to that."

YOU ARE THE WRONG KIND OF SPONTANEOUS

Dr. Allen, "People who react emotionally, without thinking first, are spontaneous. And while some people adore spontaneity, here's the problem: total spontaneity produces chaos. Self-discipline actually allows you to experience the best of spontaneity."

This image might help: Say you want to go diving to see sharks up close. Some self discipline, or boundaries, like a cage will make the experience far more enjoyable than shark watching without a cage.

So Dr. Allen recommends that by all means, enjoy your spontaneous nature, but consider using some self-discipline, or boundaries, "If you know the boundaries of your relationship, whether it's your mother, your father, your lover, your boyfriend, your kid, whoever it is... if you know your boundaries; what you want and don't want from a relationship, you are basically safer."

<u>YOU TOLERATE SITUATIONS AND PEOPLE</u>

Dr. Allen believes you can't change other people, but you can change your reaction to them.

If you're dealing with a difficult situation or with difficult people, you have one of 3 options:

- You can accept the situation or person exactly as they are.
- You can reject the situation or the person, as in avoid them or leave.
- Or you can tolerate them/the situation. (Not a great choice.)

Dr. Allen, "I highly recommend you either accept or reject, but never tolerate. Here's why: When you tolerate a person or a situation, what you're doing is half accepting and half rejecting. Toleration puts you in a stressful situation, and when that happens, your body produces the chemical cortisol. Anybody know what cortisol is? Cortisol is distress. Cortisol is the overabundant production of adrenaline. And cortisol rots in your body, it strips your nerves, ruins your T cells, will make you ill, and can, in extreme cases, actually kill you. Listen to what I'm going to say...

I do not need to like, or approve of those I love and accept. But I must love and accept everyone's right to be right or wrong.

Some people may be too toxic for you to be with, especially if you're emotionally healthy. If you put a toxic person and a well person in a room, what will you end up with? Two toxics, because the toxic person weighs a thousand pounds emotionally and a well person weighs a hundred. Toxic people will crush you. Get away from toxic people.

We therapists work for years to be able to be in the same space with a toxic person and they get us anyway. It's egotistical to think you can handle a toxic person."

YOU ARE VERBALLY GAMING PEOPLE OR GETTING GAMED

Dr. Allen is a big fan of Dr. Eric Berne's work. He's a psychiatrist who wrote the best seller "Games People Play." One of Berne's students, Steve Karpman, created a unique "Drama Triangle" that quickly identifies communication games people play. The theory goes like this: instead of communicating effectively, people take on one of three roles: victim, persecutor or rescuer in order to get their needs met.

See if any of Dr. Allen's examples sound like you, or someone you know.

VICTIMS

Kick Me: People who say things like, "This always happen to me." To which Dr. Allen responds, "You know why it always happens to you? Because you haven't learned the lesson, and you're not open to learning."

I'm stupid: This is a person who just doesn't want to learn.

Wooden Leg: Someone who makes excuses for not learning, as in "Oh, I have a ____ (fill in the blank) so I can't do that."

Harried: Someone who overloads their day so they can't do anything well.

Poor me: Toxic people who play on your sympathy.

Addict: People who are alcoholics, bulimics, or addicts of any kind.

PERSECUTORS

NIGYSOB: Translation: someone who delights in the emotion, "Now I got you, you son of a bitch!"

Blemish finders: The kind of people who would say something like, "I can't marry you, you're too short."

Courtroom: People with a controlling attitude of, "I'll decide what's right and wrong."

If it weren't for you: Accusatory people who says things like, "If it weren't for you, I'd be a doctor by now."

Passive aggressive: Someone who might say, "See what you made me do? I hit you, now I'm in jail and it's your fault!"

RESCUERS

I'm only trying to help you: Someone who uses this phrase the minute you question them.

What would you do/be without me: Attention seekers who need constant affirmation.

They'll be glad they knew me after I die of a heart attack: Drama queens who use guilt to make you appreciate them.

Once you start identifying these 'mind games' that people (or maybe you?) play, and stop playing them, the more effective you'll be at communicating.

YOU DON'T USE THE ONE WORD EVERY WOMAN NEEDS TO KNOW

Dr. Allen, "What's the only word that a woman needs to know? NO. If you want to live on the planet, ladies, you've got to know how to say no. All the women in the room, raise your right hand and repeat after me...

'I promise, on my honor, to say NO to immoral, unethical, and illegal treatment. So help me God.'"

YOU DON'T KNOW THE ANTIDOTES TO THE 5 CURSES OF MANKIND

Dr. Allen has adapted her '5 curses' premise from the work of another great therapist, Taibi Kahler.

- Curse number One is: Be perfect. I like to think of this as suicide training. If that message is in your head, here's the antidote: Be excellent.

- The Second curse of mankind: Try harder. Got one? Get two, got two? Get three. The antidote: Know what's enough.

- The Third curse: Hurry up. Anybody got a hurry up? Don't work easy, hurry, hurry, hurry. The antidote: Work easy.

- The Fourth curse: Oh this is a good one, churches love this one. Please other people first. The antidote to that is please yourself first.

- And the Fifth curse is: Be strong. You know what be strong is? Unteachable. The antidote to this is to be open. Unteachable people are absolutely lost souls. Run away from them. They are so toxic. Demonstrate a life but don't try to educate them.

YOU DON'T SAY WHAT YOU MEAN OR MEAN WHAT YOU SAY

One of Dr. Allen's favorite phrases is, "Don't SHOULD on me!" Here's her explanation:

"I recommend you don't use the phrases:
You should...
You ought...
You must ...
You have to...

Instead, use these:
I want...
I do not want...
I want you...
I don't want you...

Using the first set of phrases, 'You should, you ought to, you must, you have to,' does not make for effective communication. And I'm not just talking about you talking with other people. I'm talking about you talking to yourself as well, internal or external communication. Remember, you are listening too, the kid inside of you is listening to what you say!

Try using the second set of phrases: 'I want, I do not want, I want you and I don't want you' instead. Once you start speaking like this, you can't practice the 5 curses of mankind. Using these words will keep you anchored in what you really want and don't want.

How many people think that saying, "I don't want to!" is impolite or negative? We gotta get over that! Potency outranks politeness. Put politeness at the end of your sentence, 'I want... may I?'

If you communicate in a clean way, if you clean up your internal and external languaging, you will be able to re-wire your brain and attract what you want in life, and/or eliminate what or who you don't want in your life."

PRIVATE SESSION EXCERPTS

ANGELINA

Angelina is an attractive 30-something management executive who's dating but can't find 'the one.' This is her first appointment with Dr. Allen.

"Is your question about your health, your career or your relationships?" Dr. Allen begins, "I like to start off by finding which of the 3 is off kilter."

She gives Angelina the following examples.

- Health issues reflect your physical state.
- Career or job issues relate to your mental state.
- Relationship concerns reveal your emotional state.

"So tell me which one you're here for today," says Dr. Allen.

Angelina takes a deep breath, "Relationship, so I guess it's my emotional state. I'm having trouble with an old boyfriend who wants me to have an affair right before his wedding."

"Sounds like he wants you for a mistress," says Dr. Allen.

"Yeah, and instead of really just standing my ground and saying, 'No, you know, that's not ok with me, I'm not gonna be the one to sabotage your marriage,' I was really flaccid in my language with him and I wanted to still be liked by him. I haven't slept with him, but why was I so lame? And why am I even thinking about it, I should have said no." Angelina slumps in her chair.

"You didn't want to be abandoned, it felt good to have his attention and desire." Dr. Allen replies.

A look of recognition comes over Angelina's face, "Yeah...that's so true, huh?"

"Let me ask you this, how many times have you really, really been able to set boundaries around a man when he wants to be close, warm, intimate, and loving to you?" asks Dr. Allen.

Angelina says quietly, "I'm not good at that..."

"So what you're saying is you're now willing *not* to have him, to *not* please him, in order to have you!" Dr. Allen continues, "You want to raise your consciousness."

Angelina lets that sink in for a minute, then looks up excitedly, "Exactly, normally I'd just let him control the situation, and I realize I don't like this dynamic. But why do I still play those games, why am I even tempted?"

Dr. Allen replies, "Temptation is not wrong, it's what you do about it. It's ok to have any feeling you want, it's what you do with it that counts."

Angelina scrambles for a pen, "Let me write that down!"

Dr. Allen closes out the session with this zinger, "I want you to not fantasize relationships with men who are not eligible, Don't have a floaty boundary list. Qualify the buyer differently now. It's time to put away the toys of a child, and move into womanhood. Decide what you want and don't want and make a positive decision about that. It's called being a grown up."

Angelina appreciates the 'tough talk' approach and replies, "Thank you Dr. Allen. I needed someone to tell me the truth about my situation."

YOLANDA

One of Dr. Allen's most loyal patients is a lovely, diminutive Hispanic woman, Yolanda. "I just want to say that I was bounced around a lot as a kid. And when I found you Dr. Allen, I felt like I found a new planet."

Dr. Allen remembers, "You told me in one of our first sessions, that you weren't raised in a cozy little warm Mommy Daddy environment."

"No. I was raised in an orphanage." Yolanda says.

Instead of exuding sympathy, Dr. Allen puts a more helpful positive spin on a rough situation, "That's a real survivor training program!"

Yolanda laughs, "Very true! I had some good grandparents around once in awhile, but I also had people around that were not as good, doing things to me they shouldn't have, so I had to adapt in order to survive."

"And what is it you've learned that's helped you survive?" Dr. Allen asks. "How did therapy help you?"

Yolanda is quick to answer, "I've learned from you that 'no' is a good thing. You made me practice saying it every time I saw you. And now it comes so easy to me. I wish I'd known that when I was little. But I thank God I've learned it now. I hope this doesn't sound too dramatic, but really, it's saved me from so much pain, just that one word: No."

Dr Allen replies with conviction, "No is a darn good thing!"

JESSICA AND DANNY

Jessica and Danny are in Dr. Allen's office because of Danny's temper and Jessica's bad habit of being late. Jessica explains that Danny blew up at her the other night. She was an hour late for the dinner he'd made, and when he called her, he unleashed a verbal tirade.

The couple is barely speaking, and Jessica knows Danny will explode again, "He called me a f*** asshole and told me I ruined his evening, and we didn't talk for days."

Dr. Allen tells the couple that when it comes to Danny's temper, he did the feel, react, think routine. She suggests he try a rational response instead: Try to feel his anger, think about what he wants (and doesn't want from Jessica) and THEN he should respond to the situation.

Jessica, on the other hand, has some options as well. She can avoid these situations by being on time, or, try this radical approach: just accept that he has a temper.

"You mean he doesn't have to change, and not be so verbally abusive?" asks an incredulous Angelina.

Dr. Allen replies, "Remember, you can't change other people, you can only change your reaction to them. Accept, reject, but don't tolerate. You're tolerating him right now and it's driving you crazy. Decide if you'll accept him as he is, or leave him."

Jessica sits back and ponders this concept. She's intrigued to have a label for what she's been doing, which is tolerating the behavior. She likes the simple concept of either rejecting him, or accepting him as he is. Maybe that will bring her some relief.

Danny, meanwhile, is feeling like the bad guy again. He knows his reaction to Jessica was emotional, and not rational, and he doesn't want to lose her, "She doesn't deserve to be treated that way," he says sheepishly, "I really am sorry."

Surprisingly, Dr. Allen doesn't let him off the hook with that statement, "Lots of people say sorry. Like a parrot: sorry, sorry, sorry. How about you say sorry, and add 'I'll try to do better the next time.' And then follow through and show with your actions that you mean this."

Danny is taken aback, but appreciates the cold truth of the matter. He grabs Jessica's hand and tells her not just that he's sorry, but that he'll try to do better. Jessica says she will accept him today, and she takes Danny's hand.

At least for the moment they are accepting each other with their shortcomings, instead of just tolerating the situation, progress!

ELENA

Elena is 45 and in Dr. Allen's office because of issues with her mother, "I feel like I'm a bad daughter, and I really wish I had a better relationship with my mom."

Dr. Allen asks for more information, "What do you mean? Give me examples."

Elena replies, "Well, I've never really gotten along with my mother, and she makes me feel guilty for not doing more for her. She's always criticizing me, wants me to come over, do chores for her, but when I do, within five minutes we're arguing. I could go on and on..."

Elena spends the next half hour relaying a very dysfunctional mother- daughter relationship.

Dr. Allen lets her finish, then says, "I got news for you, that's not your mother you're dealing with, that's a toxic person. If it were your mother she would act like a mother. She may be ill, or insane or just flat out evil. But she's not in her mother role."

Elena looks strangely relieved. She was expecting to hear that she was being a bad daughter, and the fact that Dr. Allen is validating something she's known but has never been able to verbalize is liberating. "So I don't have to always do what she says, or go over when I don't feel like it?"

Dr. Allen cautions, "What I say to you is this: be very careful, and when you do go over there, treat it as if you're going near an infectious person, do you see? Be very defended, do not be vulnerable. But I don't think I'd be around her very much. Unless of course, you're willing to pay the price of going down."

Elena is stunned. She's never considered this before. Dr. Allen has just given her a new framework, and it feels right to her. She can love and accept her mother, but doesn't need to like her, and she can choose when and where to be with her mother on her own terms. A breakthrough moment.

Dr. Allen closes the session with this wisdom, "Remember: You do not need to like or approve of those you love and accept. You still have to love and accept them...which you can do, from a distance. But you don't need to be around people you don't like or don't approve of."

MALLORY

Mallory is in her mid 40's, has been dating a man for almost a year and wants a commitment and a ring. But she's having a tough time asking for it. When she brings up the subject of marriage, her boyfriend always cuts her off.

Dr. Allen begins the session, "How would it feel to say to him, 'I'm not comfortable being intimate with you without some type of commitment'?"

Mallory replies, "It would feel like I'm being, I don't know, harsh or something."

"But see, you are not asking for what you want. You get close, but you back away," Dr. Allen continues, "You're being evasive, which is one of the signs of a communication loser. You're not saying the words: I want a commitment."

Mallory looks sad, "I know, and I'm very aware that I do that."

Dr. Allen advises her, "I want you to see the complex in you that says, 'Don't ask for what you want.' Try it right now, try saying what you want, pretend he's here in the room."

Mallory begins, "Well, Adam I think we should talk about our future, and what our relationship is."

Dr. Allen is patient, "Interesting, the most important thing does not come out of your mouth. Try it again, this time use the words: I want."

Mallory can't do it, "Ok, Adam, I think it would be great..."

Dr. Allen is smiling as she throws up her hands, "Oh my goodness! OK, let me try to give you the words, then you repeat them exactly as I say them: 'Adam, I feel great about being with you but I want a ring and a commitment to show we're on the same page and have a plan for the future."

Mallory, squirming: "Oh God, I'd love to say that, but, well, Ok, here it goes, 'Adam, I want a ring and a commitment to show we're on the same page.'"

Dr. Allen quickly asks, "Now, how did that feel?"

Mallory finally has a smile on her face, "Weird, but kinda good! I so need to learn how to talk like that."

Dr. Allen, "You may need to write it out, practice in front of a mirror, kind of like fake it till you make it. Rehearse the words until you get comfortable with them. Remember the good feeling of saying what you mean. But keep practicing, otherwise your old script of not asking for what you want will come out."

Mallory promises to use her new verbal skills, and calls Dr. Allen 3 weeks later to let her know that she and Adam are engaged.

Beware of your thoughts, they become words.
Beware of words, they become habits.
Beware of habits; they become your character, your destiny at the bank, the hospital, the doctor's office, and in every relationship.

-Dr. Pat Allen

CHAPTER 2: WHY DON'T I HAVE A GREAT RELATIONSHIP?

Excerpt from a Dr. Allen stage show filled with single people:

"How many people in this room want to be respected first in a relationship? (About a third of the room raises their hands.) You're called yang. How many people want to be cherished first? (More hands go up.) You're called yin. And how many people want to be cherished and respected? (The majority raises their hands.) You're called clients!"

Laughter fills the auditorium.

"So have we got my first major peaceful loving thought? You can have it all but not at the same time if you want to be in a relationship with someone and make it work."

The hallmark of Dr. Allen's decades of therapy is her theory of how to make relationships work. As she likes to say, she may be politically incorrect with her approach, but scientifically accurate.

It's a bit of a learning curve to really understand the energy system philosophy, but as client after client will testify, once you 'get it' you'll have the magic key to the best love of your life.

So with that in mind, perhaps you don't have a great relationship because...

YOU ARE UNAWARE OF THE ENERGY SYSTEMS THAT EXIST IN RELATIONSHIPS

Dr. Allen believes that relationships are most successful when there's an exchange of complementary energies, meaning female (yin) and male energy (yang). One of each type of energy in a partnership works best.

One of the basic tenets to keep in mind about Dr. Allen's energy systems is that while the traditional male role model is considered yang, and the traditional female role model is yin, it's not purely gender based.

"I refuse to indicate yin or yang by genitals. It's an energy system. There are yin men and yin women. There are yang men and yang women. Doesn't matter if you're straight, gay, lesbian, doesn't matter. But if you want to be in a committed relationship, you've gotta decide which side of you, the yin or yang, is going to mate. That's the biggest issue."

So, how do you know which energy you are? You are:

Yang, or male energy if you like:

- GIVING
- PROTECTING
- CHERISHING

Yin, or female energy if you prefer to be:

- RECEPTIVE
- AVAILABLE
- RESPECTING

Dr. Allen cautions, "If you like giving, if you like protecting, if you like cherishing are you yin or yang? Yang! And who will you partner best with? A yin. If you go with another yang, and you don't know this principal, you will fight. You will fight."

Some more indicators of which energy system you are:

You are the male (or yang) energy if you want your thinking respected first. You feel more comfortable saying things like "I think, and I want."

You are the female energy (or yin) if you want your feelings cherished first. You're more comfortable saying things like "I feel and I don't want."

Now, are you supposed to stay in only one energy or the other? No, every person has both female (receiving) and male (protecting and giving) energy in them. You may use one kind of energy at work, another in your personal relationships. (Note that you can switch energies in your romantic relationships, but do so with awareness, negotiation and permission.)

Here's an interesting example, do you think that nurturing is male or female energy? You may immediately think it's female, since mothers have such a nurturing instinct. But nurturing is actually male, or yang energy, because it's giving, protecting and cherishing.

In any good parenting relationship, the parents are the yang energy. Yet with your partner, you may be the feminine energy.

Hence, different energies for different relationships.

YOU DON'T KNOW THE ABSOLUTELY SUCCESSFUL "5-SECOND FLIRT TECHNIQUE"

Dr. Allen's take on flirting, "You need a great deal of courage to flirt, and you can't be afraid of rejection or abandonment. It's for the brave of heart only. But it works. Your skin will blotch, you'll sweat, your stomach will turn over and you may get a headache. The body is saying 'Please, no, this is scary!' Rise above it! Flirt anyway! It's fun once you get past the fear of it."

Dr. Allen believes you'll have the best flirting success if you do it according to the energy systems.

If you are the male energy (yang) looking for a compatible partner, then you approach someone and speak first.

If you're the female energy (yin) Pat suggests you attract someone just by smiling and looking at them, but let them approach and speak to you first.

Practice flirting so you can get comfortable with the technique, maybe hang out at a populated place, like an airport where people come and go, and just try holding someone's gaze for a full 5 seconds, a signal to them you are interested. Most people look away after 3 seconds, it's those extra two that will get someone's attention and indicate your interest.

YOU DON'T KNOW THAT THERE ARE 3 DIFFERENT KINDS OF DATING

Dr. Allen believes there are three different kinds of dating.

- Duty Dating®
- real dating
- courtship

"Duty dating" is when you are trying out dating skills, it's not based on chemistry. It's practicing. While you're duty dating, Dr. Allen recommends that you date at least three different people at a time, for at least three dates each, unless they are repulsive, immoral, unethical or illegal. Or, as Dr. Allen puts it, "Date them three times unless they are wearing an orange jumpsuit with a number on the back." Why the 3 times 3 dates? She says it takes seeing someone in different situations to really get to know them.

As for "real dating," that's when you are mutually attracted to someone and you go out.

"Courtship" is advanced dating, when you know you are looking for a relationship and both parties are looking to mate.

THE CHEMICAL OXYTOCIN IS RULING YOUR LOVE LIFE

Oxytocin is a powerful 'feel good' hormone that's released when women have sex or become physically intimate with a man. It's also known as the 'bonding' hormone. Young women, especially teens, confuse this chemical reaction with love, and often think it's the guy they crave, when it's actually just the oxytocin rush.

Because of this dynamic, Dr. Allen cautions women, "It's especially important to know what the deal is before you have sex, don't commit premature monogamy. That's what happens when women are under the influence of oxytocin. You're quick to attach to someone who you don't even know. Think about this: a sociopath can screw your brains out before you even know he's a sociopath or she's a gold-digger. Get to know someone before you bond and commit."

She also recommends getting a commitment before you have sex that bonds, she calls this an "entrance" fee. For your health and sanity, she suggests you find out your partner's plans for the relationship's longevity, exclusivity and continuity.

"The worst dating deal in town is when you don't talk about what's happening between the two of you. You might believe you're falling in love while the guy is thinking you two are just friendly sex partners. Be careful who you have sex with, you may become so bonded you won't be able to pull away and get a better man."

As for men?

Men don't release bonding hormones until they're older, and in a phase knows as post andropause, so having sex is far less complicated for them when they are young.

Dr. Allen points out, "If you're a guy, have you ever had a woman who won't leave you alone after you've had casual sex? Could be because she's bonded to you. She wants more of that oxytocin rush."

YOU ARE CONFUSING GREAT SEX WITH GREAT LOVE

Be really clear on the difference between making love and having sex.

As Dr. Allen says, "Sex is a physical event, making love is a physical, emotional and mental event. People who make love can have sex, but people who are addicted to sex, rarely make love. So I teach women, and sensitive men, don't make love until you know what the deal is, otherwise, you will get hurt. I mean if it's a shipboard romance, fine, a one night stand, great, I'm not a moralist, but if you're looking to marriage and he's into a quickie, that's a bad deal."

For men, if you have sex with a woman and you have different goals (she wants a relationship, you just want sex), you may have to watch that woman disintegrate in front of you; suicide threats, forever phone calls, other life interruptions. She thinks there was an implied agreement, "But we had sex!" she cries. Avoid this by being clear with a woman, "I like you, and want to play with you, but I don't want a commitment."

A famous Dr. Allen quote, "Men fall in love with virtue, not vaginas. Boys like cheap, free sex. But boys don't fall in love even when they get cheap, free sex, they just get addicted."

YOU HAVEN'T DETOXED FROM YOUR LAST RELATIONSHIP

This applies to people who are in their yin, or feminine energy. Dr. Allen has what she calls an 8-week oxytocin detox theory, which goes like this:

If you've broken up with someone, don't contact them or call them for a full 8 weeks, because it takes that long to begin detoxing chemically and mentally from them.

You begin de-bonding chemically from someone within the first three days, but it usually takes at least two months, and sometimes as long as 2 years. To de-bond chemically from someone, you need to not hear, taste, touch or smell or see the other person. Do not get into conversations, because if you do have any kind of contact, you risk rebonding.

"Ladies, don't risk the oxytocin rush by calling him up. No excuses. Don't do it. If he calls, and catches you, you say 'Thanks so much for wanting to be friends, but I'm not comfortable with and don't want to have a platonic relationship. Next time you're interested, bring me a commitment and a ring. You've done this back and forth thing before, and I'm not willing to go through this again. I want to avoid you.'"

Once you've lasted the 8 weeks, you'll be able to see more clearly if it was the oxytocin rush you were craving, or the person.

YOU HAVEN'T TAKEN A DR. ALLEN PLEDGE

These are the well-loved pledges Dr. Allen uses in her seminars:

Women (or yin energy people), this is your pledge:

"I promise, on my honor, never, will I let that magic wand in, anywhere it can get in... unless I negotiate with its owner first about his long term plans for me, his sexual and social monogamy and his weekly continuity. And should I let that magic wand in, without a contract, I will not complain about the money I will spend on shrinks, and the time it takes me to detox. So help me God."

Men (or yang energy people), this is for you:

"I promise, on my honor, not to take my magic wand and put it in anywhere it can get in unless I tell her my goals first. I also promise, on my honor, to give, to protect, to cherish: women, kids, animals, and the planet even when they're illogical, irrational and irritating. So help me God."

PRIVATE SESSION EXCERPTS

RON

Ron is a political consultant in his 30's. He's looking to get married and start a family. He met a smart, good-looking news reporter at a convention, asked for her number and a few days later, called to ask her out. Ron says he invited her to his favorite local restaurant, and she told him she'd rather go somewhere else and maybe even do something else instead of dinner, like go see a movie. He was a bit taken aback, but took her to the restaurant of her choice. The date wasn't great.

Dr. Allen explains how two energy systems were in conflict in this situation. The reporter was using yang energy, saying 'I want... to go here." Ron was also in his yang energy, and wanted his way of thinking respected, but that didn't happen. The two yangs were clashing, or, as Dr. Allen so succinctly put it, "She was trying to take over your whole date, and you were now her bitch!"

Dr. Allen illustrates her theory during one of her seminars filled with thousands of people, "How many guys in the room would love it if a woman respected you enough to follow your leadership? How many would like that?"

Nearly every one of the over 500 men in the audience raised their hands.

"Do you see that ladies? If you do that, they'll cherish you. It happens, they fill up and it's wonderful. If you ladies want to be cherished, you've got to pick a man you respect and follow him unless he's immoral, unethical or illegal."

NICKI

"So are you a career woman, or a woman with a career?"

Dr. Allen's question makes newly engaged Nicki pause for a moment.

Nicki is a successful career woman who is used to employing her male energy in the workplace, and in her personal relationships. She's trying to learn Dr. Allen's energy system, and wants to be in her feminine energy in her new relationship.

She and her fiancée aren't living together yet, but spend a lot of time at each other's houses, and it's driving Nicki nuts. She wants to be "available and respectful" in her relationship, but needs some time to work and be alone.

Dr. Allen points out that a 'career woman' would make work a priority, but a 'woman with a career' needs to respect the relationship. The solution lies in negotiating.

"Do I stay at his house whenever he wants me there, or can I just go home and do my work? I'm tired of dragging stuff back and forth," asks Nicki.

Dr. Allen responds, "Why haven't you discussed this with him?"

"I thought yin women should just receive and, as you always say 'keep your yang mouth shut,'" Nicki replies.

Dr. Allen points out, "You don't need to be a doormat. It's perfectly okay to negotiate with him about how you divide your time. What is it that you want?"

Nicki is unsure, "I don't know, I just know I'm not really happy when I'm with him and need to get my own stuff done."

Dr. Allen tries a different question, "All right, then let me ask you this, what is it you don't want. It's often easier for women to figure out what they don't want."

Nicki instantly answers, "Oh my Gosh, you're so right, I know exactly what I don't want, I don't want the headaches and hassles of going back and forth, I don't want to be confused anymore."

"Then negotiate with love and decide how you two will spend your personal time." Dr. Allen has this advice, "Figure out a schedule that feels right to you. Ask him what he wants, tell him what you want and don't want and then negotiate from there."

Nicki looks relieved, and 3 months later called Dr. Allen for an update. She's a far better negotiator and manager of her time now, "Why didn't I do this sooner, it's so great to ask for what you want and negotiate!"

*Note: Some people might feel this approach is politically incorrect, given the strides that the women's rights movement has made for female independence. But as Dr. Allen says, the energy system philosophy is scientifically accurate. It's ok to be in your yang energy at work, but to be in a relationship, you need to have compatible energy. She likes to remind yang women to, "Leave your plastic balls at work!"

JOSH

Josh is a handsome and seemingly together 45-year-old who recently lost his job and broke up with a long time love. It couldn't have come at a worse time. He just celebrated his first year of sobriety. He also never fulfilled his dream of becoming an employed musician, and has had 'jobs' but not a career he loves.

Dr. Allen starts the session. "Let's deal with the unemployment part first. Instead of ruminating and obsessing about being fired, look at it this way, maybe you've been booted upstairs. Maybe now you can try for a career in the music world instead of a job. I want you to set a goal. Tell me, how much money do you want coming in next year?"

Josh thinks and says, "Well, I guess I'd like unlimited amounts of money coming in."

Dr. Allen, "Unlimited? There is no such thing as unlimited amounts of money. Evasiveness is not a good characteristic. Give me a specific dollar amount."

Josh dutifully corrects himself, "Ok, I would like to be making 100 thousand dollars next year."

"Would like, or want? Big difference." Dr. Allen is on a roll, "Say two guys are looking at your car that's for sale. One says, 'I would like to buy it', and the other says, 'I want to buy it.' Who's gonna buy it? The guy saying I WANT!"

Josh is totally on board with this line of thinking, grateful for Dr. Allen's direction as she prods him, "So *now* how much money do you want coming in next year?"

He laughs, and says with gusto, "I want 500 thousand coming in."

Dr. Allen continues, " So here's your plan. You say to yourself, 'I want 500 thousand dollars coming in next year, and it's ok if I don't get it, if reality doesn't give it to me. But saying "I want" allows you to be more focused, and approach life from your yang energy, male side."

Josh started using his yang energy, and it boosted his confidence. He didn't make that 500 thousand, but he did land his first paying job playing his guitar for corporate events.

ELLEN

Ellen, a widow in her sixties, is feeling extremely lonely; it's been 3 years since her husband died. She has no clue how to go about finding a relationship. " I think I'm at a point where I've just now discovered I do want to have a life after my husband died. Before, I was a little pile of clay, now I think I do want to fall in love again. But how do I meet people?"

Dr. Allen doesn't miss a beat, "You flirt!"

Ellen quickly replies, "But I don't know how to flirt!"

Dr. Allen lays it out, "Here's the deal, if you want to attract a man, look him in the eyes, then smile. But here's a trick. Look for 5 seconds. Most people look away after 3. Keep looking and smile. It feels horribly uncomfortable at first, but it gets the job done. Men think if you look 'em in the eye and don't turn away you're interested sexually."

Ellen giggles, as Dr. Allen continues, "Think of it this way, you can have the best house in the world for sale, but if you're not marketing it, no one's gonna buy it. So get out and practice flirting and let people know you're available."

Ellen is now laughing, "Aren't I too old for this? Who's going to like me, I'm 66!"

Dr. Allen dismisses that logic, "I choose to believe there's a lid for every pot. Plus you have the #1 quality that men are attracted to, so use it."

Ellen is perplexed: "I do?"

Dr. Allen reveals, "Men are extremely attracted to happy women. You are, by nature, a positive happy woman who's just come out of a dark time. Use your smile and go flirt."

Ellen leaves the office smiling, and reports back two weeks later. She flirted, attracted a man, and went out on her first date in 40 years.

CAROLINE

Caroline would love to get married. She considers herself a serial monogamist, and is confused by Dr. Allen's suggestion to date 3 people at a time, " I feel it's unethical to date a bunch of people at the same time."

Dr. Allen: "I'm not saying you sleep with 'em – just date them! Here's why. When you date just one person at a time, you are over-committed, you do your pretzel number trying to fit into their world. Dating just 2 people is an either or situation, it's competitive. But dating 3 is diversification and when you have diversity you give yourself the option of saying, 'Oh, he didn't call but the other one did,' so it lightens the inevitable rejection load somewhat."

Caroline is intrigued, "But what do I say when they want to have sex, like on the 2nd or 3rd date? It seems like there's always pressure to have sex right around that time."

Dr. Allen cautions: "Tell him women bond chemically with men when they have sex, and you want to protect yourself and not bond with men who may not end up being relationship material. It's in your best interest to protect yourself."

This simple wisdom made a lot of sense to Caroline, so she decided to get out of her monogamous dating routine.

She was able to attract and go out with 3 different guys at once, not sleeping with any of them. 2 years later, Caroline ended up marrying one of the 3 guys she had in her dating circle, someone she never would have let into her world if she hadn't followed Dr. Allen's advice to diversify.

ZOE

Zoe is a beautiful 30 year-old baby nurse. She decided to try the yang energy system and asked out a colleague, a doctor. Turns out he was married. Zoe was crushed, and is telling Dr. Allen she feels like an idiot now.

Dr. Allen sees it differently, "So you've been rejected by a nice man, and that hurts. But look at it this way, maybe you've been kicked upstairs to get a better man. But why did you put all your eggs in one basket? Where are the 2 other guys on your plate?"

Zoe confides, "I have a hard time getting past the second date with people who ask me out. They want to get romantic...and I'm not that into them."

Dr. Allen, "You need to learn how to say 'I'm not ready for that, I don't want to get sexual until we both want monogamy and continuity and are ready to mate and marry one day. I don't want to use you or lead you on'. That's the point of duty dating, to learn how to handle situations like guys who come after you sexually. Next time try saying 'No thanks' with a smile when they come after you. No explanation needed. If you don't learn to say that, to say what you mean, you'll avoid dating. Think of duty dating as something developmentally necessary for you – you'll get through these guys to get to the one you want."

Zoe started duty dating and learned how to handle various situation with words, as opposed to avoidance. She told Dr. Allen she feels like she's getting to be a pro at dating, and will be able to pick a good man out of the bunch instead of letting a guy seduce her into a relationship.

JULIA

Julia is a sweet and super cute 27-year-old who has been going out with hot guys for years, but isn't finding love.

Dr. Allen begins the session, "So, are you duty dating? Going out three times with the guy?"

Julia squirms, "Ah, not really. I mean I can tell within 5 minutes if I'm attracted to a guy or not. There is this one really cute guy I have a crush on. He has a girlfriend. But he's always flirting with me and complaining about her so I kind of want to see where it might go with him."

Dr. Allen chooses her words carefully "Two issues, first, you're telling me you want to go after someone who's clearly unavailable. Do you really want to go out with a man who's made a commitment to another woman, yet flirts with you?"

Julia, "But I'm so attracted to him!"

Dr. Allen, "And that hasn't worked for you in the last 7 years, has it? You choose men who aren't available, you pick them with your eyes, and you still don't have a relationship!"

Julia lets that truth sink in.

Dr. Allen continues, "Here's the other issue. You will have more success in getting a real relationship if you pick someone with your ears. Try going out with at least one guy with your ears, and date him at least three times. Let me tell you a secret, the guys you pick with ears, the guys who really listen to you, and say things that make you feel special, are more likely to cherish you, and are usually more moral and ethical than the guys you pick with your eyes. Bottom line, they are more committable and frankly, they get cuter the more you let them love you."

Julia is intrigued, and promises to pick at least one guy with her ears. 3 months later, she was finally in a great relationship with a guy she wasn't wild about on her first date, he really did 'get cuter' and she really did fall in love!

FARRAH

Farrah is a 43-year-old single mother whose greatest wish is to be in a wonderful relationship. She is desperate, "I'm having difficulty meeting men and frankly, even if I could find one, I'm a single mom and don't have much time."

Dr. Allen isn't buying any of it. "I only ask people to make an effort once a week, maybe a two hour event, like tea or coffee."

Farrah is still resisting. "But I don't even know where to go to meet a guy. I don't know where the hunting grounds are these days for single moms!"

Dr. Allen has a solution, "I'll tell you where your hunting grounds are, they are wherever you smile the most."

Farah laughs, "But I smile all the time, and I don't see anyone lining up to date me!"

Dr. Allen patiently continues, "What I'm talking about is that you go where you are happiest, where you enjoy yourself most. Bookstores, coffee shops, soccer games, old movie screenings, whatever. Wherever you are the happiest is where you flirt and then you will attract a yang man."

Farrah finally gives up the 'not gonna happen' attitude and agrees to try Dr. Allen's approach. She returned to see Dr. Allen months later and was happy to report that although she wasn't in a relationship, she was duty dating successfully, and no longer depressed about her relationship future.

JASMIN

It's not easy for Jasmin, she's been trying to detox from her last love. She broke off the relationship because her guy would only call her once a week, and their one date night on the weekends wasn't enough for her. She negotiated with him, and he agreed to call and see her more, but he never followed through. Jasmin is into the 4th week of the 8 weeks Dr. Allen says are needed to break an oxytocin bond. Jasmin is lonely and miserable.

Dr. Allen begins, "So you're abstaining from him, detoxing, because you want the oxytocin to go down and you want to fall out of love with him physically."

Jasmin nods in agreement, "I thought that's what I wanted, but now I'm wondering if I ended the relationship prematurely. I miss what we had so much."

Dr. Allen boomerangs the question back, "I don't know if you ended the relationship prematurely, only you can say. So did you?"

Jasmin is confused, "I mean, maybe I did end it prematurely, but I didn't know what else to do to get through to him. The way it was going was unacceptable to me."

Dr. Allen digs deeper, "What exactly was unacceptable?"

Jasmin is very clear on this issue, "It was him drifting and staying away from me for 5, 6, 7 days."

Dr. Allen clarifies, "You mean he was neglecting you?"

"Yes, exactly!" Jasmin feels vindicated. "But now I'm thinking about calling him."

"Ok, what's happening now is that you are waffling. You told me 4 weeks ago you wanted to detox. Now you are not sure you did the right thing, and you want to call him." Dr. Allen reframes Jasmin's desire to call, "So in essence, by contacting him before the 8 weeks are up, all you are really saying is, "OK, I think I'll come and get you little boy."

Jasmin is stymied, "I don't want to chase him but I want to let him know once a week is not enough time for me."

Dr. Allen is relentless, "But you already said that to him. You can't call somebody you haven't seen for 4 weeks and basically say, 'by the way I'm not going to see you.' He'll say I'm already not seeing you! It doesn't fit. I have no problem with you changing your mind about your energy system. If you want to be yang instead of yin, then call him."

Jasmin remembers her original desire, "No, I want to be the feminine energy. I want him to be a man and grow up and come after me and see me more than once a week. But why is it so painful right now?"

Dr. Allen explains, "Because you've got a few weeks to go. Oxytocin detox is at its worst about halfway through the 8 weeks. You are really missing someone you physically love. Your body likes him even if your brain knows he's not good for you."

Jasmin feels centered again, "Well I do love him, but I think I'm going to wait 8 weeks so I can see if it's really him or just the chemical rush I get that I'm missing."

Dr. Allen smiles, "Good. Remember, the sperm chases the egg. Not the egg the sperm."

Jasmin sighs, " I know that, I have to be reminded of that."

"You've got four weeks to go, the last two are the toughest." Dr. Allen asks, "So is your contract with yourself today to stand firm?"

"Yes, I'm tired of leading." Jasmin is sad, but determined.

Dr. Allen has a suggestion, "While you are detoxing, you may want to get two more men on your plate, you know, duty date."

Jasmin ponders the option, "I guess, if it will help. It's not really what I want, but I need to do that."

Jasmin called Dr. Allen 5 weeks later to inform her that her ex had called, just like Dr. Allen predicts many men will after 8 weeks, and that he was willing to do whatever he needed to get her back. She turned him down. Turns out one of Jasmin's "duty dates" developed into a fun relationship that she wants to pursue, "My new guy can't seem to get enough of me!"

KATHY

Kathy is having a tough time with a man she's been involved with off an on for a few years. He wants sex without a commitment. She wants a commitment but hasn't been able to communicate that fact. The couple is at a crossroads with a date planned "to discuss things."

Dr. Allen queries, "So when he comes to you and says, 'I want to date, make love, etc' what will you say?"

Kathy thinks a moment, "Umm, ok?"

Dr. Allen offers this advice instead, "How would it feel to do this? First, you say thank you. Thanks for the offer. That's called respecting a man. We have to respect them so they can cherish us. If we expect them to cherish us first, without respect, then their name is daddy, as in sugar daddy. So if he said 'I want to date you,' say thank you."

Kathy, "But what about the whole commitment thing, which is what I want, how do I bring that up?"

Dr. Allen guides her, "That comes right after the thank you. Here's what you could say, 'Thanks, but I'm not comfortable being intimate with you without some type of commitment."

"But he's going to accuse me of manipulating him, and playing games by withholding sex!" Kathy is confused.

Dr. Allen explains, "You can tell him you are protecting yourself, because women bond chemically when they have sex, and that the next time you bond with someone you want it to be in a loving, committed relationship. That's your virtue, and that's what men fall in love with and propose to."

Kathy looks relieved, "That feels better, I think I can say that."

Kathy was surprised by the results of being upfront and requesting a commitment. She came back a few months later to tell Dr. Allen this technique really helps her weed out 'the losers!"

CHAPTER 3 BIG QUESTION: HOW CAN I TELL IF IT'S REALLY LOVE?

"The only way you know you love yourself or anybody else is by the contracts you are willing to make and keep. That's it, that's your integrity."

This is one of Dr. Allen's most loved insights. So many people struggle with the definition and meaning of love, her message makes it simple. If you love yourself, or someone else, you'll honor the commitments and contracts you've made.

One of the biggest problems in relationships, and frankly the world today, according to Dr. Allen, "Too many sloppy contracts. People aren't acting with enough integrity."

So here's how you figure out if it's really love:

UNDERSTAND THAT ALL RELATIONSHIPS GO THROUGH 4 PHASES

Dr Allen believes every relationship goes through 4 distinct phases in about a year's span. They are:

- The perfect phase
- The imperfect phase
- The negotiation phase
- The commitment phase

The perfect phase is the time when all seems amazing, you have great chemistry and you're kind to one another.

The imperfect phase is the second three months. You might start having conversations that sound like confrontations and the communication gets competitive rather than complementary. At which point you either learn to negotiate or you hire someone like Dr. Allen to help or you just split up.

The third phase, negotiation, is critical, it's what sets good relationships apart from bad ones, and it's where real intimacy is born. If you make it through this, if you build your relationship, then you reach...

Phase 4, or total commitment, which for many means an engagement or marriage.

Dr. Allen recommends you get to know someone for at least a year before marrying. As she likes to say "You don't get a termite report until you are in escrow." Think of an engagement as your escrow, and your marriage as the moving in part.

NEGOTIATE WITH LOVE

Dr. Allen says there are only three ways to deal with people:

- You intimidate them with fear (saying things like "you better do this, or else") or
- You seduce them with guilt ("If you leave, I'll do something horrible") or
- You negotiate with love.

Negotiating with love sounds like "This is what I want or don't want, what do you want or not want, let's make a deal."

Dr. Allen explains further, "Real intimacy in a relationship isn't just a great sexual connection, it's emotional intimacy – which is the ability to ask for what you want and say no to what you don't want. You negotiate with the people you care about. That's intimacy."

One of Dr. Allen's most coveted relationship tools is her "Relationship Contract." Couples who've used this, not just once but repeatedly, have far better relationships than they ever thought possible. The guide that follows helps you negotiate with your partner the 4 key areas of every relationship:

- Time (as in how much you'll spend alone, together just the two of you and as a couple socializing)
- Space (where you live, who has what responsibilities)
- Money (yours, mine and ours)
- Play (what you'll do for fun, alone and together, sexually and non sexually)

THE RELATIONSHIP CONTRACT

Write down your "wants" and "don't wants" in each of these areas, then negotiate. Compromise in case of conflict for best results!

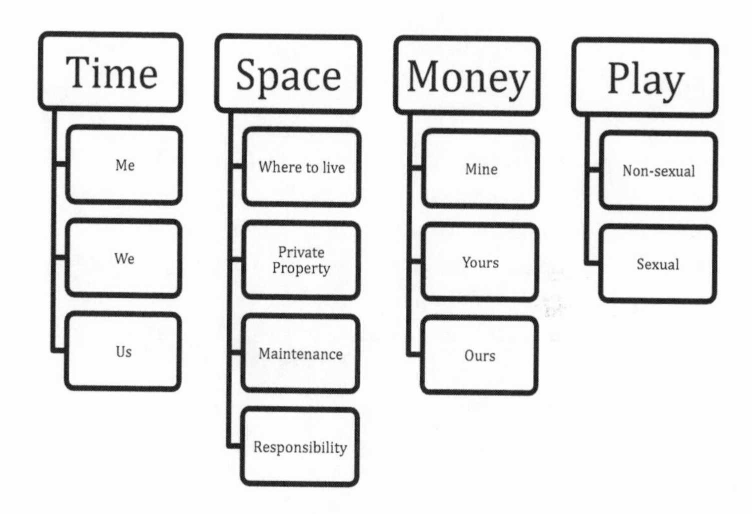

TIME

Me: Ask yourself, how much alone time do you need? As Dr. Allen likes to remind people, "You gotta be a 'Me', to be a good 'We.'"

We: How much time do you need to be with your mate? How much time would you like to spend together? A day, a week, a month? And that means no TV's, no movies. A great Dr. Allen illustration, "Don't tell me 'Oh, we go to the movies we have dates all the time.' When you're going to the movies, it's you and she or he and them on the movie screen. That's an 'Us' date, you're not focused on each other."

Us: Be careful not to confuse this with a 'we' date. Us is "we plus them," as in another couple, or doing something with your kids.

SPACE

Where to live: Decide where you will live. His house, your house, new house? Consider sleeping arrangements. "You do not have to sleep together, too much proximity dulls chemistry." As Dr. Allen has said, "A girl with apnea and a guy with restless legs syndrome cannot sleep together."

Private property: These are the pre-nuptial agreements or post-nups. Dr. Allen firmly believes these are good contracts to have. It's much easier to negotiate what would happen if you did break up while you like each other as opposed to when you hate each other during a divorce. Discuss private space, too. Determine what will be 'my closets, my drawers, your this, and your that.'

Maintenance/Responsibility: Negotiate items such as: Who's going to be responsible for the cars, the pools, the whatever. Also discuss who's going to be responsible for the chores. As Dr. Allen points out, "This doesn't necessarily mean you have to do 'em, it means you've gotta see that they're done."

MONEY

Mine, yours, ours? Decide how you'll handle your finances, as in what constitutes 'my money, your money, our money.' Ask, "Do we put all of our money in one joint account and draw out? Or do we put it in our own separate accounts and pay our bills separately, and then put some into a shared joint account?"

However you do it is ok, just have a clear plan. Dr. Allen warns: "If you have money problems, you're gonna have sex problems. If you've got sex problems, you're gonna have money problems. I guarantee it. Talk about it, deal with it, and negotiate how you'll handle the money."

PLAY

Non-sexual play: involves what you like and want to do as entertainment. Break this down further into "Me, We and Us" when you discuss. The "Me" would the category where you discuss things like drugs and alcohol use. The "We" and "Us" involves what you like to do as a couple; do you belong to a ski club, enjoy hiking, etc. and what are your expectations for these activities, as in how often do you want to do them?

Sexual play: is another hot topic and area where couples often aren't in sync. If you discuss your likes and dislikes, and what you need, want, and don't want, you'll stand a better chance of having a satisfying sex life. You'll also be able to identify trouble triggers, as Dr. Allen likes to ask, "Does anybody have any screws loose sexually?" Will you accept or reject that behavior? (Remember, tolerating is toxic.) What about flirting, porn, computer sex? Is there anything that your partner is doing that you really don't like and you know you won't be able to handle it? This is where you get real about your sex life.

Dr. Allen recommends, "This relationship contract, if you really keep it up, will make your relationship better. And here's what you do: you negotiate a contract, live with it for 2 months, upgrade it, live with the new one. Eventually, you'll be doing the negotiating a couple times a year, but I promise you, if you do, you will keep your relationship vital and alive and exciting and stimulating for life."

RECOGNIZE THE 4 DIFFERENT TYPES OF ANGER AND DEAL WITH THEM

We're all afraid of rejection, of being abandoned, and we get angry when we get threatened. But anger isn't just yelling, it rears its ugly head usually in one of 4 ways:

1. Frustration: Often child-like, as in "Why is this happening?"

2. Resentment: A much more adult type anger, as in "It's your mistake, why am I paying for it?"

3. Denial: As in "I don't think I have a problem with drinking, eating, etc." or, "I'm not angry"

4. Indignation: This is the "I'm mad as hell, I'm not going to take it any more!" kind of anger.

The way out of anger, is of course the hallmark of Dr. Allen's teachings: *Make a positive decision followed by action as soon as possible.*

"If you don't recognize your anger, if you don't deal with it, then you risk that your anger will 'come out crooked.' If the mind doesn't know it, and the mouth can not talk about it, the body will demonstrate it in illness, accidents, and other bad ways."

DO NOT TRUST YOUR PARTNER.

Dr. Allen, "I HATE the word trust. Little kids trust their parents and get beat to a pulp by them. I love the word trustWORTHY.

Replace the word trust like this: 'I'm gonna take a risk on you, to see how trustworthy you are, and I'm gonna watch how you make and keep agreements. And if the trustworthy record is good enough, I'm gonna mate and maybe marry you. But I know, absolutely, that you as a human being, may break your agreements, and then I will have to do one of two things, give up on you, or start a new trustworthy agreement.'

Trustworthiness has to be built over time, by making and keeping agreements. Trustworthiness is the foundation of love."

DO NOT COMMIT TO YOUR PARTNER

Human beings are fallible, and everyone makes mistakes. You've probably heard that often. With that in mind, Dr. Allen has a pledge for every person who wants to be in a relationship. She doesn't want you to commit to the other person, she wants you both to commit to the relationship.

Raise your hand and repeat the following pledge:

"I promise, on my honor, never will I mate or marry a fallible human being. Instead, I will commit to the relationship I want to have with a finite fallible human being, and I will do my part to make it work, and hope to God they do theirs!"

PRIVATE SESSION EXCERPTS

LISA

Lisa is a devoted Dr. Pat Allen client. Money issues are ruining her relationship, she's constantly arguing with her live-in boyfriend, who makes far less money than she does. Despite negotiating with him, they can't seem to get on track.

Lisa, frustrated, lays out the latest, "When you talk about negotiating, we've done that. We've talked about money and how we should handle it. I want to have my own account and a joint account from which to write bills. He doesn't want me to have my own account. We just totally disagree, and we keep going around and around. I'm so frustrated!"

Dr. Allen states very matter-of-factly, "You really have only two options at a juncture like this: you either compromise, or split. If you two can't negotiate a solution you both can live with, if you can't compromise, you're incompatible."

Lisa is incredulous, " So I leave a relationship over money because I refuse to put all my money in one account? Why can't he just do it my way?"

Dr. Allen explains, "That's not a compromise. You have to give a little, and he has to give a little. Maybe the compromise is you try it your way for 3 month, then his way for three months and then decide what works best for the two of you. But if either of you bully the other into submission, that person gives up themselves and their ideals for a relationship, and that relationship will never work."

Lisa tried a few more times to compromise, but the relationship eventually crumbled. She's now dating a new guy, an accountant, and they're thinking of moving in together once they get engaged. He's told her he'll do whatever she'd like to do financially, which Dr. Allen says bodes well for the relationship, because he's cherishing her feelings.

DREW AND MIRANDA

Drew is a successful businessman in his early fifties and he's had an anger management problem his whole life. Drew's girlfriend Miranda, no shrinking violet herself, wants to break up, but has agreed to come to one last session with Dr. Allen before doing so.

Dr. Allen asks, "What has the rest of the relationship been like lately?"

Miranda begins, "To be honest, it's amazing, he's just so great most of the time, funny, kind, generous... but the anger thing always creeps up."

Drew adds, "It's like we get along fine for a few weeks, and then we just implode, usually for stupid reasons where we are pressing each other's buttons."

Miranda chimes in, "I'd love to be with him, but we always seem to get into these stupid fights."

Drew adds, "And I'd like us both to acquiesce, as you've said in the past, we surrender our egos to win at the relationship. But we seem to be able to do that only a few weeks at a time."

Dr. Allen clarifies, "Maybe two weeks is your cycle. Here is the truth of the matter, you people are so volatile that you will ebb and flow and the one word you're never going to get to use with each other... is bored. You like each other, periodically. And you love each other all the time. The problem is the liking part, that's what you have to work on. If each of you considers the other to be at least 51% valuable, then you might accept the fact that you're volatile."

Miranda is agitated, "So are you saying I have to accept his outbursts?"

Dr. Allen replies, "No. You can reject him. But what you've been doing is tolerating and it's made your relationship toxic. You either accept that he has a temper, or you reject him. You are not going to change him, the only thing you have control of is how you react to him. Do you want to break up and reject him? Or is he 51% valuable and you accept him as he is?"

Miranda takes a moment to ponder this, and says softly, "He is, he is more than 51% valuable."

"Then try this," Dr. Allen says, "And make a contract with each other right now. A pledge. Hold hands please."

Drew and Miranda exchange glances, they know what's coming.

"Drew, will you look into Miranda's eyes and repeat: 'I promise to give to you, to protect you and cherish you Miranda. I promise to put your feelings ahead of mine as long as they're moral, ethical and legal.'"

Drew repeats every word emphatically.

Now it's Miranda's turn, and Dr. Allen guides her, "Now look at Drew and repeat, 'Drew, I promise to receive from you, to be available to you and to respect you as long as you are moral, ethical and legal, so help me God.'"

Both Drew and Miranda are smiling, as Dr. Allen continues: "I now pronounce you boyfriend and girlfriend."

Drew: "Amen. And thank you."

JULIE

When Julie first met Dr. Pat Allen, she was so upset at what Dr. Allen was saying about 'respecting a man, and being receptive' that Julie threw a bottle of orange juice at Dr. Allen and stomped out of the room. She returned a few weeks later after calming down.

Julie explains, "I was scared of men, and I'd fight with everyone, I was just a mess. But I was also very stubborn, and everything had to be my way."

Julie began a relationship with a great man named Bob, but that coupling fell apart just like the others. When Bob wanted to spend more time together than Julie did, she just left the relationship.

With Dr. Allen's help, Julie recognized her patterns, and learned about the art of compromise, really taking in what Dr. Allen says in every seminar, "You build a relationship by working through problems."

Julie explains how she 'grew up', "When I left Bob, I was happy at first, but after I got all my 'alone time' I was lonely. I didn't have a family...and I really had liked him."

Julie asked Bob if they could try again, and the two began seeing Dr. Allen for guidance.

Julie admits it was hard at first, "It used to drive me crazy, I was selfish. I had to admit the relationship and Bob were important to me, and I needed to work at it, to nurture the relationship and not just get my needs met."

A big breakthrough came after several meetings with Dr. Allen where the couple learned to negotiate.

Bob had called Julie and asked her to spend the weekend with him, but she had some projects to do.

Julie remembers, "My initial usual reaction was selfish and I told Bob I needed to work, because I had so much to do, and he said, 'Do whatever you want.' But I could just tell he was so disappointed."

That's when something clicked for Julie, and she remembered Dr. Allen's advice about committing to 'the relationship', and how she wanted to be 'a woman with a career' and not 'a career woman.'

"So then I thought, OK, I'll work for just one hour, then I'll take a bath, I'll take my hour and I'll become a girl. And then we can play together, remember that?"

Bob said, "I do. It seemed like such a small thing, but that's the night I finally felt like we were on the same page."

Dr. Allen describes the moment, "So it sounds like you acquiesced to each other?"

Bob and Julie, in unison, "We did, and it felt good!"

Dr. Allen points out, "That's called devotion. Devotion to the relationship. Remember, none of us are really worth marrying when you think about it. We are all individuals with a screw loose somewhere. So fitting together as a team is basically a piece of machinery, and if you do it well, if you can get all the parts to work together, you end up a unit."

Julie is beaming, "Thanks Dr. Allen, I wouldn't have this relationship without you. I wouldn't have a family!"

"The only way you know you love yourself or anybody else is by the contracts you are willing to make and keep. That's it, that's your integrity."

-Dr. Pat Allen

CHAPTER 4:
THE 20 FAQs (and Dr. Allen's answers)

1. I'M MISERABLE IN MY RELATIONSHIP. SHOULD I LEAVE?

I choose to believe that staying and investigating is a good deal. Stay till you can't stay. He or she who leaves first, repeats the same lesson.

There are only two times when I say leave:

1. When there is physical violence
2. You're getting physically ill or emotionally ill by being with that person. You're losing you.

If neither of these conditions exists, I say stay in your relationship and work through the problems, strengthen your connection. Start a trustworthy record again. I maintain the best marriages are those that survive mistakes.

2. WHAT DO I DO IF MY GUY STARES AT OTHER WOMEN?

When a man looks at a pretty woman, it's generally because his eyes are doing what he's created to do. It's like looking at a pretty picture. I would recommend to you that as long as he doesn't fall into the soup, and as long as it isn't for too long a period of time, don't be mad at your man for looking and glancing. But when he ignores you, when he cranes his neck around and neglects you, say this. "Honey, I really appreciate that you enjoyed looking at that pretty girl, but I really felt neglected and abandoned when you stopped talking, turned your back on me and paid special attention to her."

If it continues to happen, you'll have to decide if you want to accept or reject his behavior, and either stay with him or leave and get someone who's more cherishing.

3. WHAT'S THE BENEFIT OF MONOGAMY?

Family. And maintaining your integrity.

4. IS THERE JUST ONE SOUL MATE FOR ME?

No, What fit you ten years ago won't fit you this ten unless you've grown with them. For example, say you marry in your 30's and your partner didn't grow with you. Soul mates are people who are chemically compatible and communicate and grow together.

5. WHY CAN'T I GET OVER MY EX?

It may be that you are still chemically bonded, or your addiction to them may simply be a psychological need to control whatever you've ever owned before.

6. MY PARTNER IS A SLOB, SHOULD I KEEP TRYING TO CHANGE HIM?

No, but you may choose to accept him because he's 51 percent valuable. Some slobs are better than other slobs. You either accept people as they are or you reject them as they are. Because when you tolerate them you're half accepting and half rejecting.

Remember, you can't change anyone. You can negotiate mutual behavior changes, but when push comes to shove you can decide whether they're valuable enough to accept or lacking in value and you need to reject them. But you don't tolerate. Toleration is just a bomb waiting to go off inside of you.

7. WHY AM I SO ATTRACTED TO "BAD BOYS?"

Because they know what they want and don't want and they go for it. You're attracted to the power. You might get date raped, they might beat you, but some women actually enjoy the rush they get. The excitement and danger turns you on, which means you may be a norepinephrine addict. That's a hormone released in these situations, it's like adrenalin.

Good guys generally don't lie, cheat, steal, and they are not violent. Check your value system when it comes to what really turns you on.

8. HOW DO YOU ATTRACT A MAN?

By looking good. Does that mean you have to be beautiful? No. What a man sees with his eyes is a woman who loves herself. Even if she's handicapped she can have 'the look of love,' which is you doing things to show, "I am taking care of me. I'm doing what I can to be the best me I can be." That attracts men because they see a woman who loves herself, a happy woman, one who's not going to have to make her life work at the expense of his life.

Men are extremely attracted to happy women.

9. WHY DIDN'T HE CALL?

It may have nothing to do with your desirability. It simply may be that you were not what he wanted, that night, or in this lifetime, and he passed.

10. IS IT OK TO HAVE SEX ON THE FIRST DATE?

Depends on what you and the other person want. If the other person is looking for a partner, they're not gonna be impressed with a fast lay. If they're looking for a fast lay, and you are too, just make sure you have safe sex.

I'm positive you can get laid if that's what you want, but if you want to be in long term relationship, you better get to know that person, because sex alone is not going to carry a relationship into the family and cohabitating and building phases.

11. WHY IS IT SOME MEN DON'T LIKE TO TALK MUCH?

Men (yang men) want small sound bites that are respectful, meaningful, and factual. We women have double the word vocabulary that most men do. We will talk you to death...

12. I'M HAVING AN AFFAIR, DO YOU THINK I'M A TERRIBLE PERSON?

I have no moral opinion about that, that's your business. But it's an expensive way to live if you ever hope to mate or marry. If you're having an affair while you're in a marriage, you're not upholding your contract, which means you don't really love the other person or yourself. You have no integrity.

13. I'M A GUY WHO JUST WANTS TO, AS YOU SAY, "GET LAID." DOES THAT MAKE ME A BAD GUY?

No, it makes you a man. A man wants to have intercourse because he likes it. Roughly every 24 hours, because that's just the way it is. The nature of man is to be sexual. But it would be good, and I would recommend that you let the lady know what your goals are, for example, 'I'm not interested in a long term relationship but I really find you attractive and I want to play with you.' That way you're not leading her on.

14. I'M A GUY OFTEN ACCUSED OF "NOT BEING ABLE TO COMMIT." FRANKLY, I DON'T WANT TO.

You're obviously either rich, handsome, sexy or manipulative, and you are winning so many of your deals that you don't have to negotiate anything more. I choose to believe that when you meet a woman you really want, who requires you to work for it, you will be just as committable as anyone else. My guess is you're a very desirable man who wins more than you should, therefore you lose in the long run when it comes to being able to have a deep physical and emotional relationship.

15. WOMEN THINK I'M A GUY WHO'S "SO NICE", BUT THEY WON'T HAVE SEX WITH ME. WHY'S THAT?

How are you picking your women? For friendship? Very often if you're a nice guy you haven't let the woman know you're sexually interested in her. You haven't touched her. We're very sensitive to touch. We know what you're doing when you reach out to us, a pat on the arm, shoulder, whatever. We're checking out to see if we can handle your touch, then we decide yes or no and pull away or don't pull away. That's how you get to know us. It appears that you may be not signaling her that you're sexually interested. We are not mind readers, we assume if you're not doing those things, you are not sexually interested.

16. MY GIRLFRIEND DUMPED ME, I THOUGHT YOU SAID WOMEN BONDED WITH MEN WHEN THEY HAD SEX?

Yin women bond with men when they have sex, yang women don't, they are in their male energy, and if you had great sex with her, that means you got a goodie you couldn't afford. Basically she did what animals do that are very yang. She dumped you. She was off to the next one. Masculine women do not bond. They also don't orgasm, or fake them because they're too head-trippy. Masculine women either have been raised masculine or they've been abused or violated so that they've climbed up into their head and that's where they live. Their bodies do not relate, and they will not be vulnerable.

17. MY PARTNER AND I FIGHT ALL THE TIME, IS OUR RELATIONSHIP DOOMED?

Fighting is a violent word. Try using the word confront.

Here's how to communicate so you can make progress instead of creating pain. I say the first thing you do when you confront someone is to make them right for what they're doing wrong. Say, "You have every right to do what you are doing, but I am uncomfortable and I don't want that in my life. How do you feel or think about negotiating or a compromise?"

See if your partner is willing to negotiate, compromise or agree to disagree and drop the subject.

18. HOW DO I KNOW WHEN TO LEAVE A RELATIONSHIP?

I believe that the end of a relationship is when you feel apathy and empathy. You can't even get angry. You've seen this game before. You can't take it "it won't happen again" one more time. You know it will happen again. You realize you need to avoid the other person because you'll get sick. And you can practice something called "agape love," which is when you believe and say, "I release you. While I love you, I don't love you better than I love myself. You are too gamey for me to play with, live with, share my life with and I pray you get help."

19. YOU ADVISE NO SEX WITHOUT A CONTRACT IF YOU'RE LOOKING FOR A RELATIONSHIP, BUT GUYS DON'T STICK AROUND IF THEY'RE NOT GONNA GET SEX, SO WHAT DO I DO?

Tell him you bond chemically with men when you have sex, and you want to bond next with a guy you have a future with. If he leaves you, think of it this way, you'll be younger to find the right man. Men fall in love with virtues, not vaginas.

20. HOW LONG DO I STAY IN A RELATIONSHIP?

Don't stay longer than a year unless you are getting what you want from the relationship.

I also don't recommend you sign any legal agreements (marriage, mortgages, etc.) until 365 days have gone by. That's because you don't really know someone until you've been with them for at least a year. A sociopath can screw your brains out or rob you before you even know they are a sociopath.

By the way, if you're having a tough relationship that confuses you, it may be for this reason: sometimes the biggest, hardest most sensitive relationships are the most erotic and romantic ones. They require a lot of work and negotiating.

Ever wonder why cupid has arrows? Those are the issues you're having. I have a belief system that it's better to push the arrows thru than to pull them out. Practice stoicism. If you run away you're not doing your part in the relationship. He or she who leaves early repeats the mess painfully. He or she who stays till the arrow goes through goes to the next higher level.

CHAPTER 5
FAMOUS DR. PAT ALLEN GEMS

The following pages are filled with the sayings, phrases and quips Dr. Allen has dispensed over the years. Her most loyal clients and friends have been gathering these bits of wisdom for years. So here they are, compiled in one place for the first time!

FOR MEN ONLY

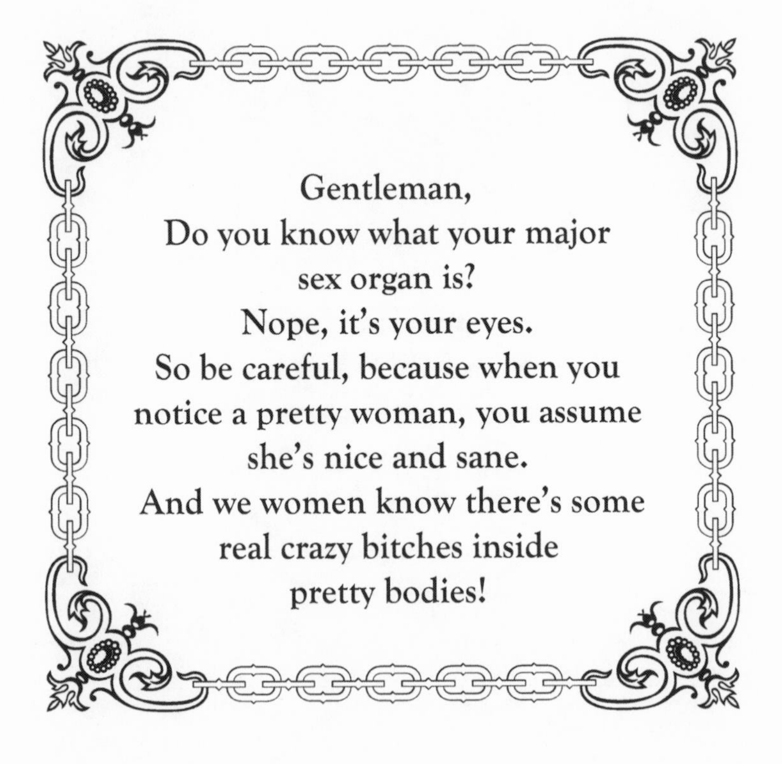

Gentleman,
Do you know what your major
sex organ is?
Nope, it's your eyes.
So be careful, because when you
notice a pretty woman, you assume
she's nice and sane.
And we women know there's some
real crazy bitches inside
pretty bodies!

Men fall in love with virtue, not vaginas.

Men speak very logically.
If they say they're not ready for a commitment,
don't argue with them.

Men, try this: Don't ask your woman,
"How can I help you?" try
"How can I help you be happy?"

Good question to ask yourself, "Do you want to be in a long term committed relationship or just play and date?"
Be upfront about your intentions.

Why do men love bitches? Because bitches require men to give and that makes guys feel like the yang men they are.

Men should not be expected to fill the role of a girlfriend. Yang men like one-sentence statements and small sound bites that are factual, meaningful and respectful.

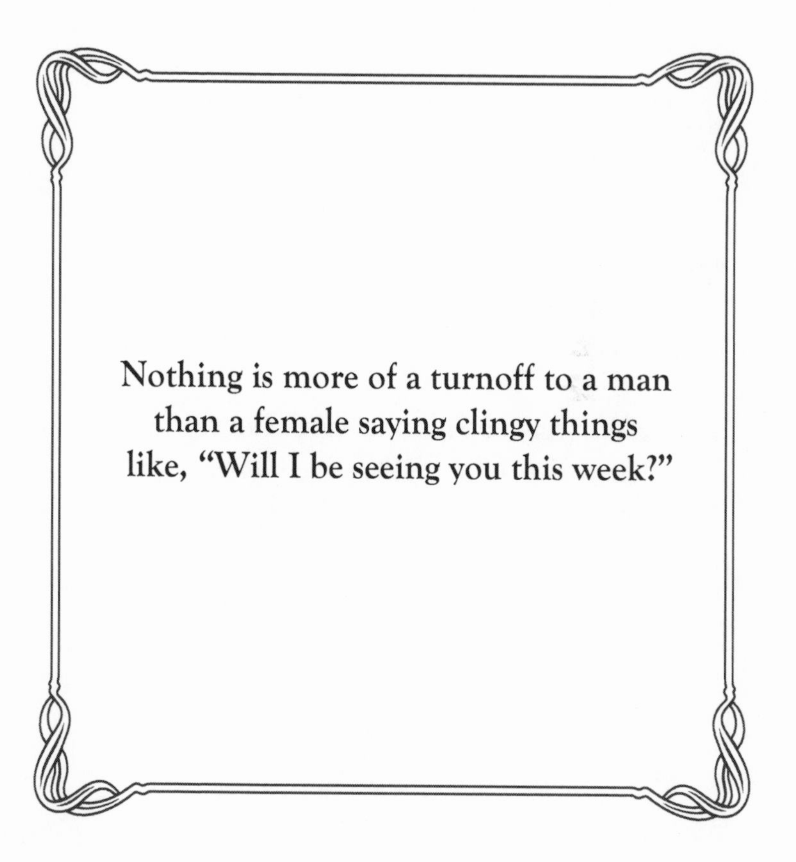

Nothing is more of a turnoff to a man than a female saying clingy things like, "Will I be seeing you this week?"

Disrespectful women drive their men into the arms of younger women.

If a woman is left unattended,
she will be stolen.

FOR WOMEN ONLY

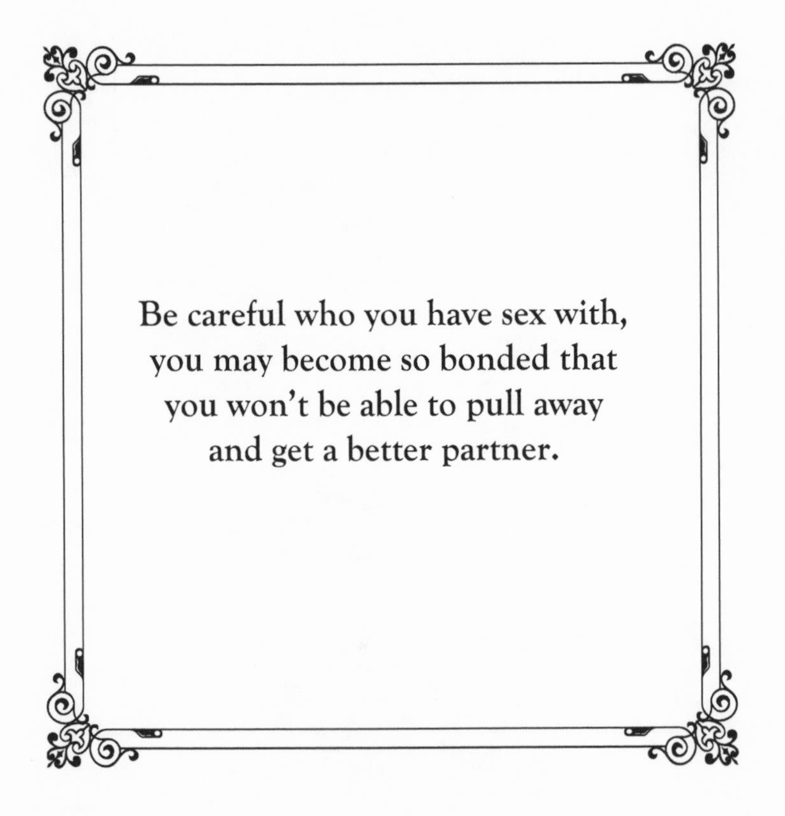

Be careful who you have sex with,
you may become so bonded that
you won't be able to pull away
and get a better partner.

Often women don't understand what cherishing means. Some women see it as being a doormat, subservient, and that you're giving away hard fought emerging power.
It's not.
It's easy to love a baby in clean diapers, it takes cherishing to love a baby in dirty diapers.

Stop being a mother to grown men.

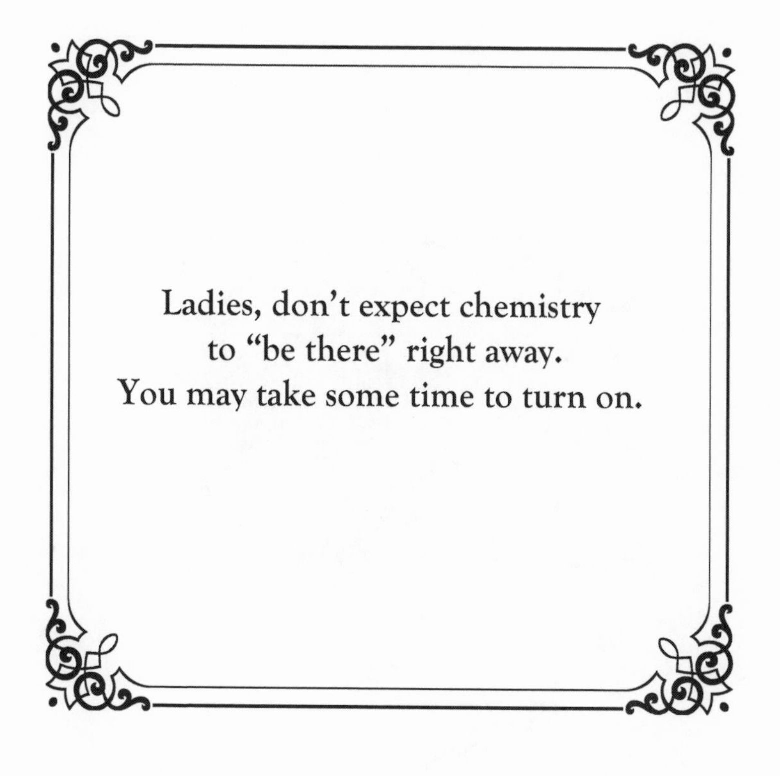

Ladies, don't expect chemistry
to "be there" right away.
You may take some time to turn on.

Pick him with your ears.

Don't try to use the energy systems at work.
At work, it's yang energy only
and all you do is negotiate.

Ladies, if he doesn't want you
within a year, move on.
Detoxing from someone is painful,
but a wasted fertile, youthful,
feminine body is not a good thing either.

Beauty is taking care of your health and cleanliness.

Marry the guy who can give you a better life than you can give yourself.

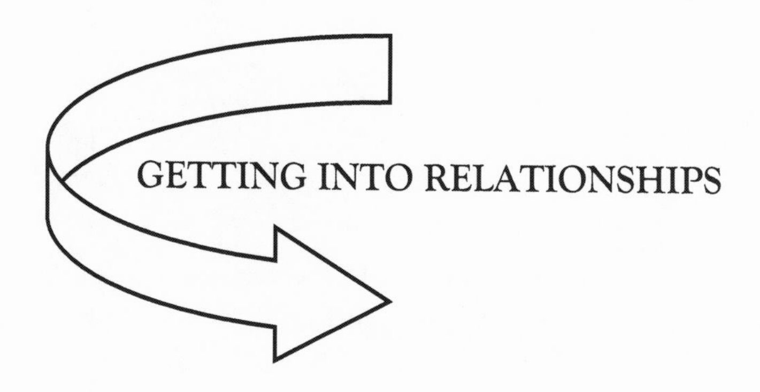

GETTING INTO RELATIONSHIPS

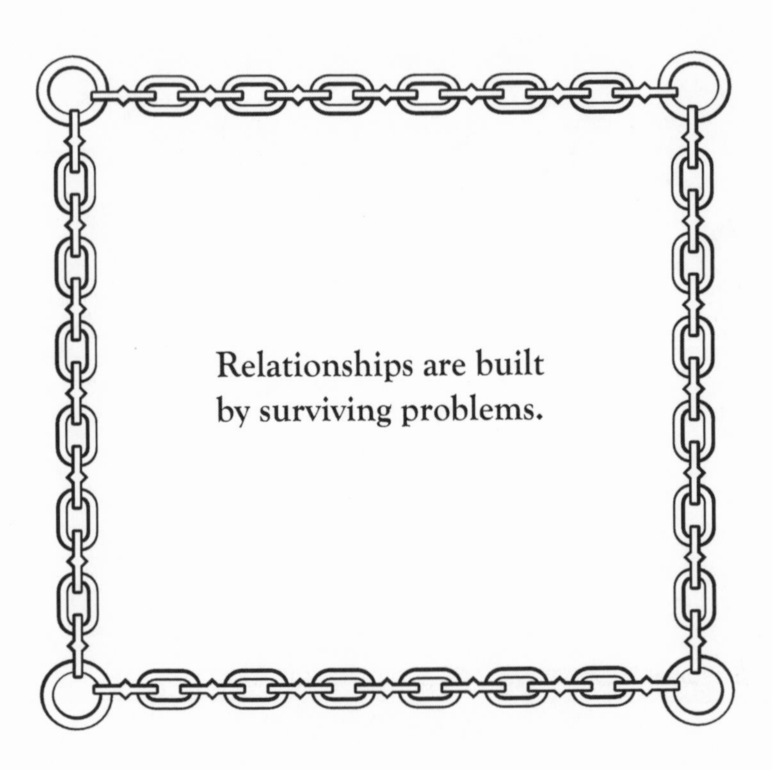
Relationships are built
by surviving problems.

When you take sex out of the equation,
do you see love?

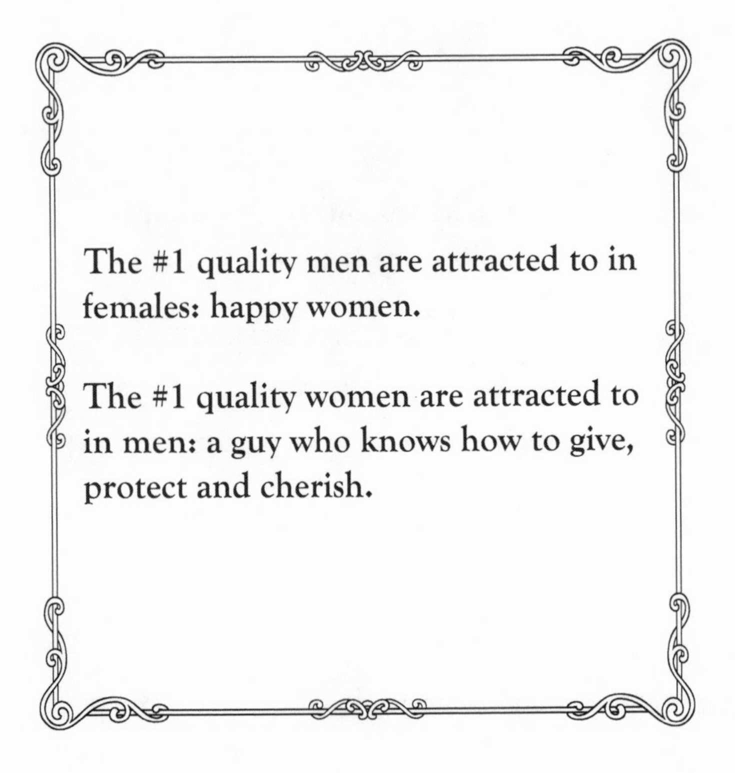

The #1 quality men are attracted to in females: happy women.

The #1 quality women are attracted to in men: a guy who knows how to give, protect and cherish.

Narcissism (being both yin and yang)
isn't bad.
It's just a state called being single.

There is a lid for every pot.

Qualify the 'buyer' (future mate) differently if you want results different from past relationships.

A false sense of intimacy produces
the same oxytocin rush
as real intimacy.

Having intercourse is a big event for a yin woman or yin man.

Why an engagement period? You don't get a termite report until you are in escrow.

If you're looking for the perfect person, get comfortable being single.

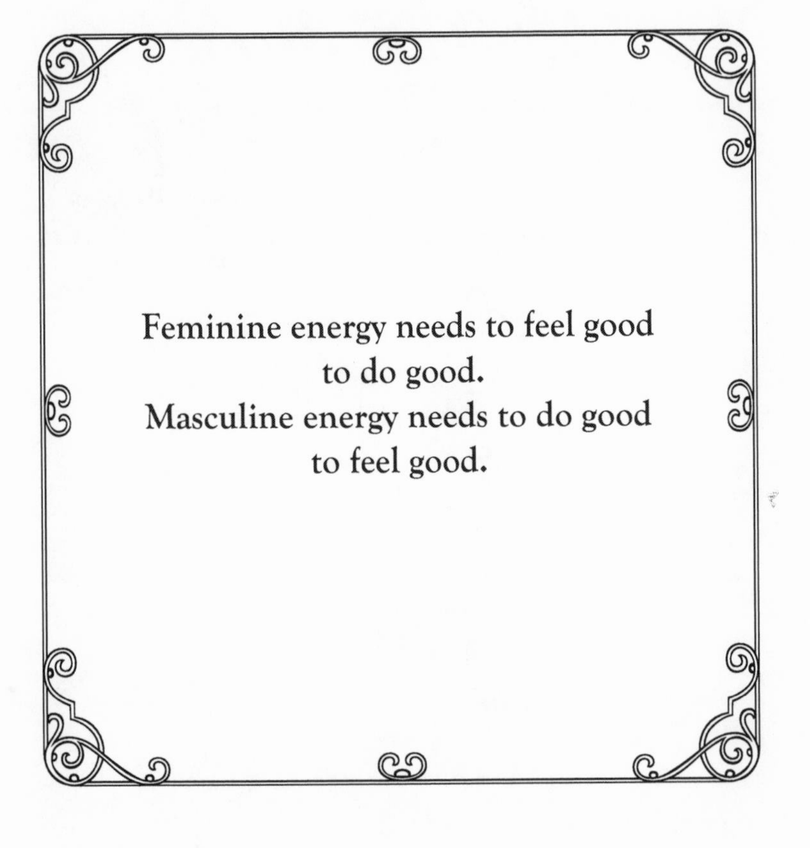

Feminine energy needs to feel good
to do good.
Masculine energy needs to do good
to feel good.

Passion is not love.
Affection is love.

It's perfectly ok to sleep in separate rooms.
With guest privileges!
Too much proximity can lower chemistry.

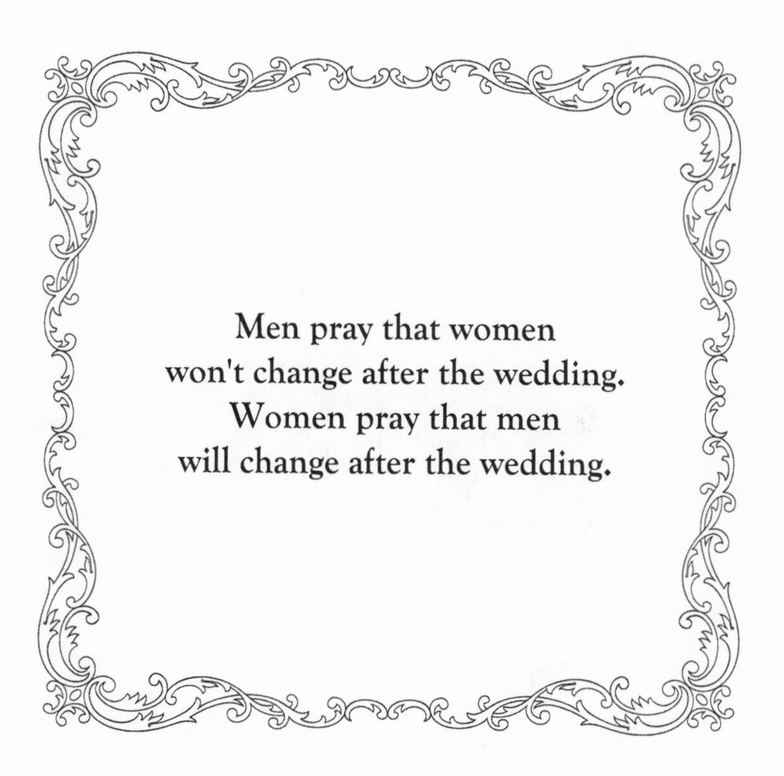

Men pray that women
won't change after the wedding.
Women pray that men
will change after the wedding.

Wait a year to get married.

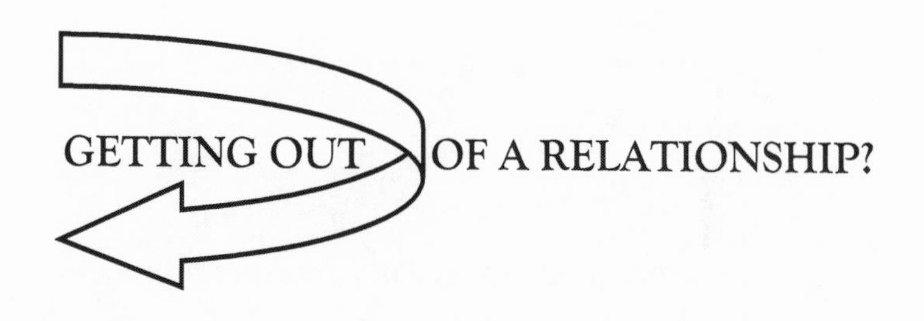

GETTING OUT OF A RELATIONSHIP?

"I don't know" really means:
"I don't want to think about it,
deal with it, or change."

If he or she is 51% valuable, stick with them.

When you're arguing, don't bring out Big Bertha: "I'm gonna divorce you, leave you." That's too heavy a price. Save that for when you're ready to hire an attorney and it's over.

Women get peace of mind by knowing
what they don't want.
Men get peace of mind by knowing
what they want.

Lovers can't be friends until they move on and have new lovers.

Don't let a good crisis go to waste.

Don't gather information
that's too painful to handle.

Don't go to a dry well for water.

Stingy and abusive people are toxic.
Stay away from them.

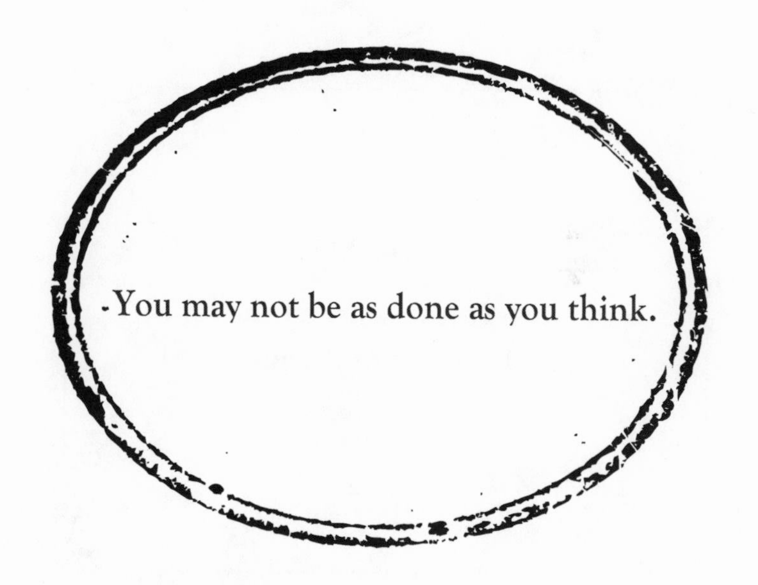
You may not be as done as you think.

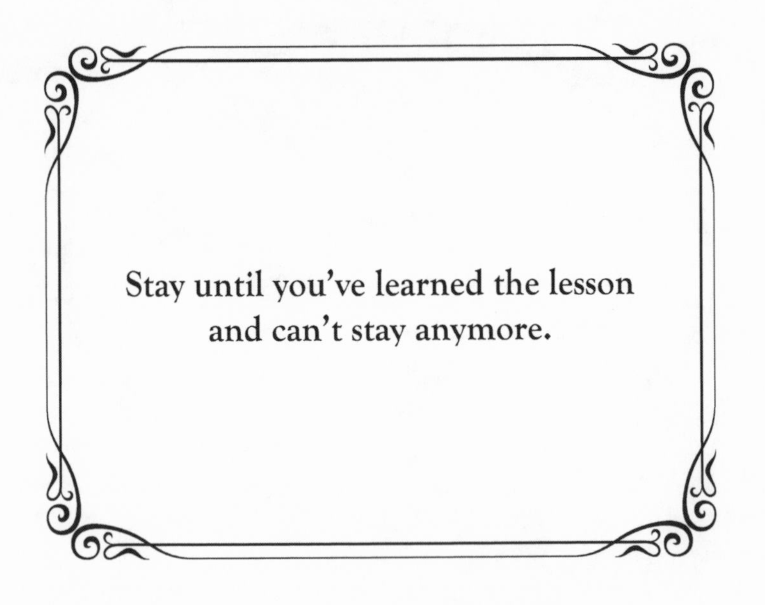
Stay until you've learned the lesson
and can't stay anymore.

Don't criticize and don't rescue.
Work on yourself.

If your partner divorces you,
you've been freed.

If you're a dumper, don't call the other person 'just to talk,' that's rude.

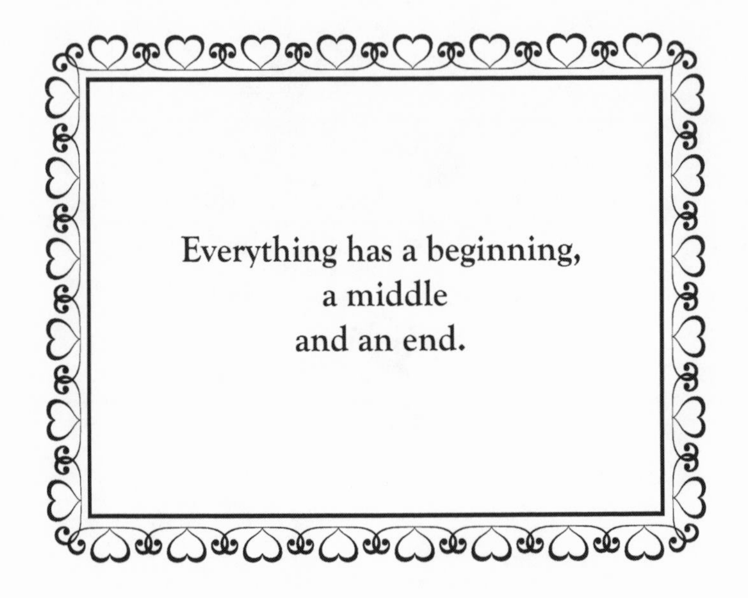
Everything has a beginning,
a middle
and an end.

LIVING AND LOVING BETTER

The only way you know you love yourself
or anybody else is by the contracts
you are willing to make and keep.

Remember, you can't change other people, but you can change your reaction to them.

What the mind does not know,
and the mouth does not say,
the body will demonstrate.

**When you're addicted,
your mind can't stop you.**

Temptation isn't wrong.
It's what you do about it that counts.

If you can't cause pain (i.e. can't say "No") you usually end up hurting yourself.

Accept, reject,
but don't tolerate.

When you feel afraid, pause, and think rationally about what action you will take or what you will stop doing.

Please yourself first. No favor goes unpunished.

"Perfect" people do what they think they should do, not what they want to do.

Feelings are not negotiable.
They just are.

There are no ‘bad’ feelings,
It’s how you act on them that counts.

Performing robots (good little girls and boys) end up in my office.

Obsession is a negative demand for that which you are not successfully negotiating for.

The problems with much of the world today are due to sloppy contracts.

Be clear with yourself, ask,
"What is it that I want or don't want?"

I do not need to like or approve
of those I love and accept.
But I must love and accept
everyone's right to be right or wrong.

If you don't drive on the right side of the road
in the USA, or the left side in England,
you will die.
(i.e. "Do the right thing!")

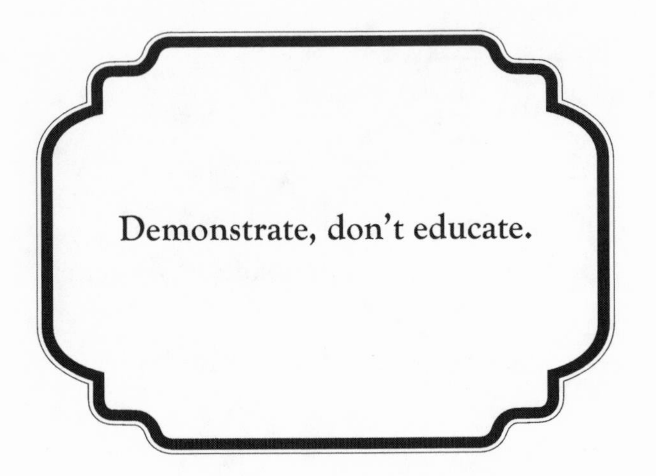
Demonstrate, don't educate.

Youth has its time. So does maturity.

Spirituality is the ability to love and be loved.

Think about what you can DO,
not how you FEEL about this situation.

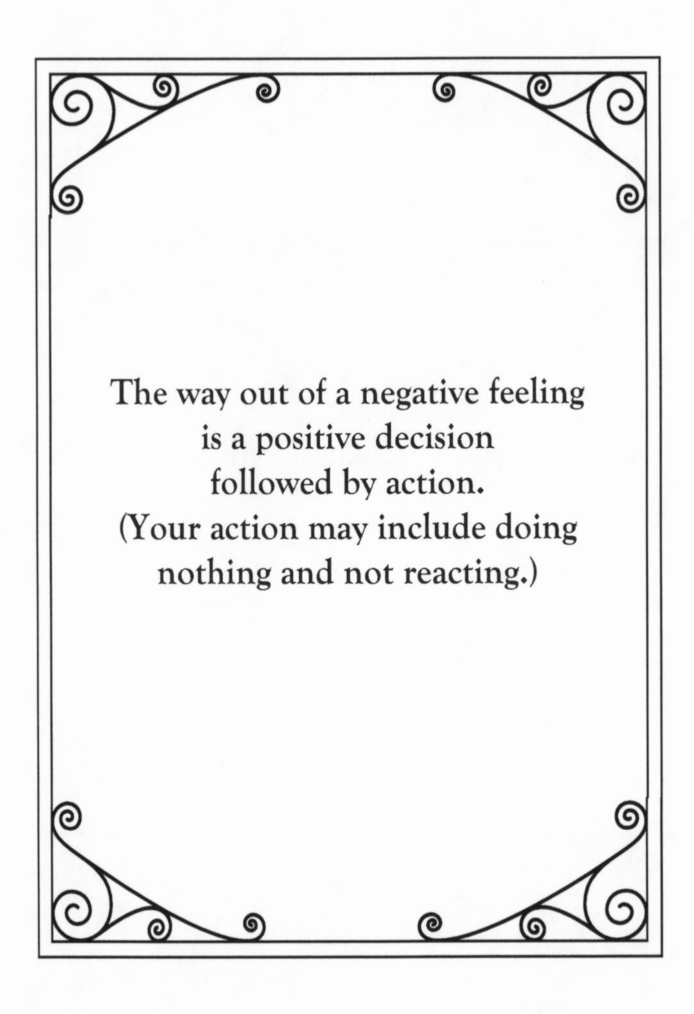

The way out of a negative feeling
is a positive decision
followed by action.
(Your action may include doing
nothing and not reacting.)

I pronounce you vulnerable and ready to fall in love with someone, even though the fear of loss may be paramount. It's called being a grown up.

THE DR. ALLEN
PLEDGES

For Women:

"I promise, on my honor, to say NO to immoral, unethical and illegal treatment.

Furthermore, I promise, on my honor, never to give, protect or cherish a healthy able-bodied human being over the age of 10 (especially men) unless I get what I want first."

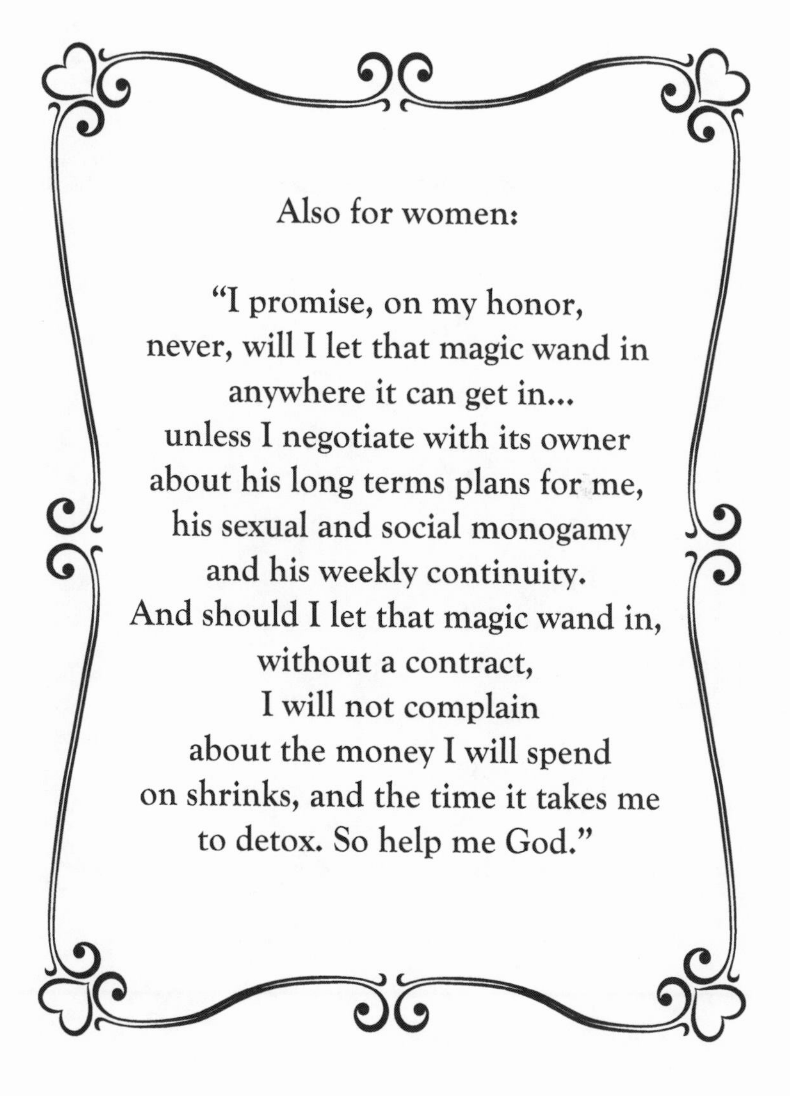

Also for women:

"I promise, on my honor,
never, will I let that magic wand in
anywhere it can get in...
unless I negotiate with its owner
about his long terms plans for me,
his sexual and social monogamy
and his weekly continuity.
And should I let that magic wand in,
without a contract,
I will not complain
about the money I will spend
on shrinks, and the time it takes me
to detox. So help me God."

For men:

"I promise, on my honor, not to put my magic wand in anywhere it can get in unless I tell her my goals first.

I also promise, on my honor, to give, to protect and to cherish women, kids, animals and the planet even when they are illogical, irrational and irritating.

So help me God."

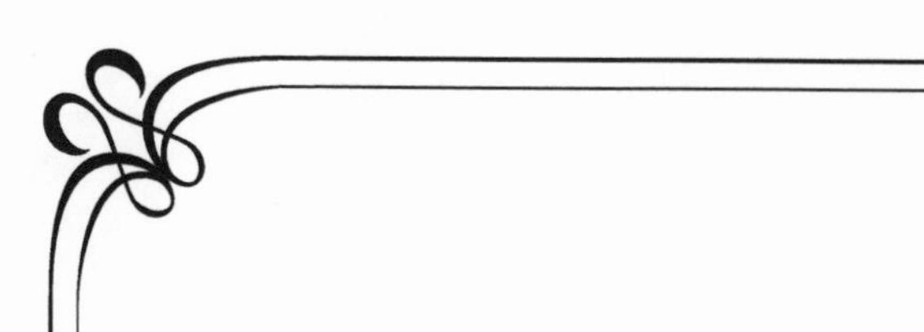

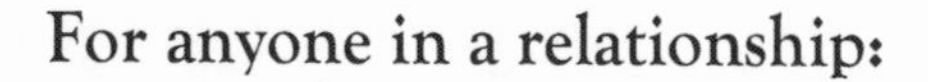

For anyone in a relationship:

"I promise, on my honor,
never will I mate or marry
a finite, fallible human being.
Instead, I will commit
to the relationship
I want to have
with a finite fallible human being,
and I will do my part to make it work,
and hope to God they do theirs!"

Dr. Pat Allen Biography

Dr. Pat Allen, PhD, is a cognitive behavioral therapist, licensed as a marriage, family and child therapist as well as a Certified Addiction Specialist. She's also an instructor level Transactional Analyst. Dr. Allen has devoted over 38 years to studying and sharing wisdom developed from years of one-on-one and couples counseling, "Life is a gift, my goal has always been to give something back."

With her trademark wit and humor, Dr. Allen has led workshops, retreats, and conducted thousands of her special Hollywood "Monday Night sessions" which look and sound like stand up improv comedy mixed with therapy. She's also the author of the best selling single girl's bible, "Getting to I Do," among other books. In addition, Dr. Allen is the co-founder of the American Depression Association and founder of "The Dr. Pat Allen WANT® Institute."

Countless people have been inspired by her teachings, and have learned how to express their wants and needs with integrity and honesty while avoiding the damaging ploys of intimidation and seduction.

TV talk shows (Oprah, The Millionaire Matchmaker) have called upon Dr. Allen for her insight and answers to life's toughest questions, and some of the world's top celebrities can be found in private sessions looking for and getting great advice on how to live and love better.

"The secret of life is having courage. May you wear out, not rust out. May you have many scars from taking risks; calculated risks."

Made in the USA
Lexington, KY
27 February 2014